A Woman's Secret to a Balanced Life

LYSA TERKEURST

SHARON JAYNES

HARVEST HOUSE PUBLISHERS

EUGENE, OREGON

A WOMEN'S SECRET TO A BALANCED LIFE
Copyright © 2004 by Lysa TerKeurst and Sharon Jaynes
Published by Harvest House Publishers
Eugene, Oregon 97402
www.harvesthousepublishers.com

Library of Congress Cataloging-in-Publication Data
Jaynes, Sharon.
  [Seven life principles for every woman]
  A woman's secret to a balanced life / Sharon Jaynes and Lysa TerKeurst.
    p. cm.
  Originally published: Chicago : Moody Press, 2001.
  Includes bibliographical references.
  ISBN-13: 978-0-7369-1402-4
  ISBN-10: 0-7369-1402-1
  1. Christian women—Religious life. I. TerKeurst, Lysa. II. Title.
  BV4527.J39 2004
  248.8'43—dc22   2004001557

Printed in the United States of America

To our mothers with love:
Louise Edwards and Linda Gardner—
we rise up and call you blessed.
Proverbs 31:28

Methods are many,
Principles are few.
Methods always change,
Principles never do.

–Source Unknown[1]

Contents

A Woman's Secret to a Balanced Life: A Bible Study

Lysa

Just as life is much more fun when shared with friends and family, so is the writing of a book. What a joy it has been writing this book with one of my best friends, Sharon. Thanks to Sharon for your never ending encouragement and love. A special thank you also needs to be given to the many others who've allowed me to share little pieces of their life stories...Sheila Mangum, Becky Peed, Daniella Russo-Gellar, Dr. and Mrs. Smith, Mike Griffin, and Katherine Hahn. Also, an extra big thank you to my sweet family who share this great adventure of life most closely with me. The love of my life, Art TerKeurst, and the three little princesses who make our life full of fun, Hope, Ashley, and Brooke. Also to my three recently adopted sons: Jackson, Mark, and Adam. What an honor it is to be your mommy. Finally, thanks to all the women who gave their time and heart to serving God through Proverbs 31 Ministries. What fun it is to be making a difference for Jesus together!

Sharon

There are many friends and family members who have touched my life and allowed me to share their lives within the pages of this book. A special thanks goes to:

My partner in ministry Lysa TerKeurst. Many say that Lysa and I are "joined at the hip" but the reality is that we are "joined at the heart." Her encouragement has helped me run the race with endurance. My mother, Louise Edwards, for allowing me to share our story of the redemptive power of Jesus Christ. Jack and Doril Henderson and Wanda Johnson for their role in leading me to the Lord. Mary Johnson for her organization inspiration. Bill and Alice Brafford, Cissy Smith, Judy Turner, Mary Marshall Young, Grace and Cindy Ely, Elizabeth Dyar, Patti Beasley, and Ernestine Nevils for sharing their stories. Cheryl Gunderson for mentoring "my girls." My husband, Steve, and my son, Steven, for their never ending love, support, and patience.

ONE

Seven Cascades

SHARON

*T*o celebrate our twentieth wedding anniversary, my husband and I traveled to Maui, where we decided to explore the tropical beauty along a road called the Hana Highway. The brochures promised black sandy beaches, a view of Hawaii's largest volcano wreathed in clouds, African tulip trees with orange-red blossoms, exotic plants tucked among bamboo forests, and vistas of raucous waves crashing against rocky cliffs.

Instead of being carted up the mountain in a cushy, air-conditioned tour bus, we decided to rent a car and travel at our own pace. After all, the tour guide from the hotel lobby informed us that it would take three to four hours to travel fifty-two miles to the road's end. Being city dwellers who move at a fairly rapid pace, we surmised that the laid-back Hawaiian was simply planning to take his time puttering up the mountainside. We were sure we could make the trip in half the time.

Mr. Tour Guide warned us, "The road is very winding and difficult to maneuver."

"It's just a sales ploy," I whispered to Steve. "We don't need a guide. Besides, if he can drive that big bus up the road, surely we can manage this little Buick."

Wiser words were never spoken! I should have had second thoughts as I passed by a T-shirt in the gift shop that read, "I survived the road to Hana."

The fifty-two-mile stretch of highway was anything but a stretch. It was as if a two-year-old had held a fat crayon in his chubby hand and scribble-scrabbled circles on a piece of paper. Then a surveyor, mistaking the twists and turns for a map, designed the road accordingly. A writer noted that calling it a highway was like calling a Volkswagen a limousine. Yes, the road offered spectacular views, but I missed many of them because my eyes were closed due to motion sickness.

Well, three and one-half nerve-wracking hours, 54 bridges (many of which were one lane), and 617 hairpin turns later, we made it to the mountain's crest and the end of the Hana Highway. Was it worth the twists and turns, cliff-hanging maneuvers, and near head-on collisions?

The sight I beheld when we reached the top will be etched forever in my mind. A series of seven interconnected pools spilled into one another down the mountain and formed the spectacular Wiamoku Falls. The rains from heaven pour into the first pool at the mountain peak. When it's filled, it spills into a majestic waterfall that ends in the second pool several yards down the mountain. The second pool overflows to a third pool, then a fourth, fifth, sixth, and seventh. Eventually, the seven waterfalls flow into the Pacific Ocean.

Those seven cascades are much like our relationship with God. When we come to Christ, God pours His blessings into us, filling us with His love, power, and grace. The more time we spend with Him, the more we become full of His love, which spills over to those around us.

As a matter of fact, Proverbs 31 provides us with seven waterfalls and pools. Lysa and I discovered that insight into Scripture as we began to work with an incredible organization called Proverbs 31 Ministries. Our desire is to help women build godly homes. We believe that the place to start is by touching a woman's heart for Christ, which in turn touches the entire family. We've identified seven qualities (or waterfalls, if you will) in the wife of noble character mentioned in Proverbs 31. With those qualities in mind, we established the Seven Principles of the Proverbs 31 Woman. The order of the principles has great significance, as we strive to keep our priorities in perspective. In our fast-paced, upside-down society, boundaries are blurred, roles are reversed, and priorities perplex us. These principles help to bring our lives into focus and to give us direction.

Now, as we share the Seven Principles of the Proverbs 31 Woman, I want you to envision yourself taking in the breathtaking plummet of the waterfalls from pool to pool. The Proverbs 31 woman:

- Reveres Jesus Christ as Lord of her life and pursues an ongoing, personal relationship with Him.

- Loves, honors, and respects her husband as the leader of the home.

- Nurtures her children and believes that motherhood is a high calling with the responsibility of shaping and molding the children who will one day define who we are as a community and a nation.

- Is a disciplined and industrious keeper of the home who creates a warm and loving environment for her family and friends.

- Contributes to the financial well-being of her household by being a faithful steward of the time and money God has entrusted to her.

- Speaks with wisdom and faithful instruction as

she mentors and supports other women and develops godly friendships.

🖉♥ Shares the love of Christ by extending her hands to help with the needs of the community.

As women, our lives must be filled, first and foremost, with Jesus Christ. Then and only then can Christ's love spill over first to our husbands, second to our children, then to our homes, our friends, our community, and the world.

On some days, the seven falls are more spectacular than on others. During heavy rains and frequent storms, God fills the pools to bursting, and water rushes grandly from one step to the next. The results are spectacular. However, no one likes being caught in a downpour.

How like our Christian walk. No one enjoys the storms of life. But it seems that during those times God fills us to overflowing, and onlookers are inspired and refreshed by the splashes of His grace displayed in our lives.

But sometimes dry periods come, when the falls are reduced to a mere trickle and appear inconsequential and insignificant. We feel we aren't much to look at, and those watching aren't "oohing" and "aahing." That's when we need to pray that He will shower us with His presence and fill us anew.

The Proverbs 31 woman has represented an ideal for women throughout the ages. While she intimidates some, all would agree she is a role model worth emulating. Scripture describes her as smart, skillful, thrifty, and strong. She's a good cook, a savvy money manager, a contributor to the community, an entrepreneur, a seamstress, a blessed mother, a faithful friend, a loyal wife, and a devotee of God. As Proverbs 31:10 states, "An excellent wife, who can find? For her worth is far above jewels." The *New International Version* calls her "a wife of noble character."

But I personally like the *Amplified* version that describes her as "a capable, intelligent, and virtuous woman." The Hebrew word that's translated "excellent" or "virtuous" can also mean "wealthy, prosperous, valiant, boldly courageous, powerful, mighty warrior."

One word I can't find listed in Proverbs 31 is the word "perfect"—what a relief. Yes, the Proverbs 31 woman is a pretty incredible ideal. She's an awesome standard of excellence. But Scripture never says she was perfect. She probably had days when she yelled at her kids for misbehaving. She probably had days when her husband kept quiet and didn't praise her at the city gates. And occasionally, I think she had days when she worked with her hands but not in delight.

Why do I think that? Because even though she was excellent and virtuous, she was a woman who needed a Savior. And that takes us right back to the top of the waterfall.

That's where our journey in this book begins, too. Lysa and I want to share with you our ongoing efforts to become Proverbs 31 women. We'll talk about our victories and failures, uncover some biblical treasures, and offer practical suggestions for becoming a woman who is filled with Christ, a woman who "spills over" for others.

So put on your hiking shoes and join Lysa and me as we explore the joys of becoming a Proverbs 31 woman.

Revere
Jesus Christ
as Lord

TWO

A Humble Respect

SHARON

*P*rinciple 1: The Proverbs 31 woman has a personal and ongoing relationship with Jesus Christ.

I love the book of Proverbs with its practical guidelines for successful living. It's not about how to be smart. It's about how to be wise. The writer provides his son with basic principles on how to lead a happy and prosperous life and begins right at the top of the waterfall, "The fear of the Lord is the beginning of knowledge" (Proverbs 1:7).

Interestingly, Proverbs' life lessons quickly turn to the subject of women. Being the mother of a teenage son, I'm sitting in the background shouting, "Amen! Amen!" But just as the book opens with how a "bad" woman can cause misery and pain, it ends with instructions on how a "good" woman causes joy and prosperity. It begins with a father encouraging his son to seek the fear of the Lord as the source of knowledge and ends with a mother instructing him that "charm is deceptive, and beauty is fleeting; but a woman who fears the LORD is to be praised" (Proverbs 31:30 NIV).

The "fear" mentioned here doesn't mean we're to be afraid or terrified of God. It means we trust Him and cultivate a humble respect, an admiring awe, and a holy reverence for

Him. King Lemuel (who was the fellow whose mom offered the advice on a good woman) was told, "Son, if you can find a woman like that, you will have found a treasure worth more than rubies."

The first principle of the Proverbs 31 woman states: The Proverbs 31 woman reveres Jesus Christ as Lord of her life and pursues a personal and ongoing relationship with Him. Now, lest you get confused because you've scoured verses 10-31 and can't find Jesus' name mentioned anywhere, let's think about who the Proverbs 31 woman was.

She lived before Christ's time. Because she loved the Lord, she would have been a woman who waited with great anticipation for the predicted Messiah. Of course, the Messiah did come, but long after the Proverbs 31 woman. So while she looked forward to the Messiah and fervently loved God as she did so, we have the privilege of knowing Jesus and loving Him.

Of course, none of us was born with this love inbred. We each fell "in love" with Christ in different ways. In this section, we will pause at the first waterfall to consider how we can deepen our relationship with Christ. And the best place to start is by remembering how that relationship began.

One thing I love about traveling and meeting new people is listening to their stories. Everybody has one. You have a story, your neighbor has a story, and I have a story. Maybe you became a Christian when you were four years old and have been inching steadily closer to the Lord for the past fifty years. Praise the Lord for your story. Maybe you ran away from home when you were fifteen years old, became addicted to cocaine, and came to Christ through a social worker in a jail cell. Praise the Lord for your story.

As we stick our toes into the warm water of Pool 1, Lysa will tell her story, I'll tell mine, and we'll look at some specific ways to love Jesus more. So join us now at poolside.

THREE

Picture Perfect

LYSA

*S*ince a picture is supposed to be worth a thousand words, I'm going to show you some snapshots of pivotal points in my life. Here's the first:

Click!
High and Lifted Up

The first memory I have as a young child is being lifted onto my father's shoulders as he carried me to the front of a crowd of people. He put me down on some kind of a stage where, at the age of two, I recited the Pledge of Allegiance. There I stood, as my proud parents and others watched this little curly-headed toddler recite words like "republic" and "indivisible."

This was a good time for our family. My dad had just returned home from being stationed in Korea. I was the center of my mom's world, as most of her days were spent caring for and playing with me.

When I was four, my sister Angee was born. While at first she was an unwelcome intruder in my life, I soon began to love her in my own way. I especially enjoyed making her eat the gourmet mud pies (made with genuine dirt) I whipped up in my little pretend kitchen. These memories bring back feelings of love and security from my childhood...feelings that would soon be shattered.

Click!
The Little Window Just Out of Reach

When I was eight years old, I stayed with my grandmother for the summer. I was thrilled at the idea of riding on an airplane and having a fun vacation. And the summer did start out great. We went sightseeing and made lots of visits to a large toy store. We went to church together, and one Sunday I gave my heart to Jesus. My grandmother bought me a Bible and read me its wonderful stories.

But things stopped being so great when my grandmother became sick and frequently had to visit her doctor. She would leave me in the care of her neighbor, who was a trusted friend.

My grandmother did not know it, but this man had terrible problems and started to sexually abuse me. He told me this needed to be "our little secret," and if I ever told anyone, my mother would die. I was terrified. I wanted to tell my mom, but the thought of losing her was unbearable.

I desperately wanted to escape each time my grandmother dropped me off at his house. I knew my only chance for escape was when I went to the bathroom. There a little window on the back wall was always left open. I remember thinking if I were just a little taller I could climb through that window.

For three summers I lived through this nightmare. During that time, I never grew tall enough to reach the little window.

Click!
Tragedy on Bedford Way

Middle school was a time of great turmoil for me. I wasn't considered cool enough to be accepted into the in crowd. The curls that were so cute at age two prevented me from wearing my hair in the popular style, and our limited finances didn't allow for the latest fashion statements. All that, combined with being clumsy, made my dreams of being accepted by my peers impossible. To make matters worse, the secrets that were locked in my heart were killing me.

Then, one day I came home from school, and Daddy was gone. He never came back.

I couldn't hold back all my pain. With tears streaming down my face, I told my mom my horrible secret. I begged her not to die, and she assured me she wouldn't. She did the best thing a mother could do in that situation. She believed me and assured me we would get through this together.

The little blue and white house on Bedford Way looked so peaceful and picture perfect on the outside. The house was intact, but the family was torn apart.

Click!
The Little Gold Ring

I still remember wondering what phone call could ever be so important that my mom would want to sleep with the phone. We called him Prince Charles. He was the man of my mom's dreams, and they were in love. The Christmas after their engagement, Charles presented me with a small, beautifully wrapped box. Inside was a little gold ring with my birthstone. He had given my mom a ring as a token of his love and devotion, and now he had given me one, too. I now had a daddy who loved me! I asked if I could call him "Daddy," and he said yes. It was one of the best Christmases ever.

Soon afterward we celebrated the big wedding. It was great living in a home where my mom and dad loved each other. Then, just a couple of years later, a second sister, Sarah, was born. Life seemed good once more.

Click!
The Broken Stick Figure

The woman's office had fancy degrees hanging on the wall and expensive-looking furniture. I wondered if she had some kind of special glue with which she could repair my heart. During my second year of high school, my biological dad called the state's social services department and reported that he had raped me during one of our weekend visits. Now this therapist's job was to get to the bottom of this big mess. She asked me to draw a picture that represented how I was feeling. I don't remember what I drew, but I do remember how I felt—rejected and ashamed.

Why had my dad said those things? They weren't true. What was so wrong with me that my own dad would reject me in such a shameful way?

I wished that one day some man would love and accept me. I knew my mom and stepfather loved me, but I still had a void that needed to be filled.

Click!
Our Little Angel

I was the only girl in my senior class who had to have her date stop by the maternity ward on the way to the prom. My mom had just given birth to sister #3. Haley was beautiful. She had thick black hair and big blue eyes. I loved my little sister, and we developed a special bond.

But during my freshman year at college, my mom called to tell me Haley was sick, very sick. That next summer Haley underwent a liver transplant. Slowly, she seemed to get better. I was reluctant to return to school for my sophomore year, but everyone seemed encouraged by Haley's progress and felt she was well on her way to recovery.

Just a few weeks after I went back to school, Mom called to say Haley had taken a turn for the worse and was now with Jesus. My heart sank, my eyes welled up with tears, and my body felt lifeless as I hung up the phone and dropped to my knees.

I had felt betrayed by a lot of people in my life, but now I felt betrayed by God. How could He have let her die?

As soon as I got home, I went to the funeral home to tell Haley good-bye. When I walked into the room where her body was, I realized she was gone. No more giggles and wet kisses. No more silly grins and peek-a-boos. Good-bye, my sweet angel, good-bye.

Click!
The Big, Pink Church

I was angry at God. I told Him I had tried life His way, and I didn't like how things had turned out so now I was going to live my way. I finished college and acquired my first job. Life seemed good on the outside, but I was lonely. I thought my loneliness was due to a recent break-up with a boyfriend, so I reasoned that if I could just find another boyfriend, I'd feel better.

One Saturday my roommate came into my room holding up a large ad in the newspaper for a big, pink church. She told me that at such a big church I probably could find some really nice friends...maybe even a boyfriend.

I attended church for the first time in a long while the next day. I did find some really great friends, so I started to attend regularly. But I was careful only to let people get so close for fear they would find out about all the junk from my past. I wanted to be a good Christian and part of that meant being perfect, right?

Click!
Hearts, Flowers, and Stars

I still remember where I was sitting when the phone rang. My friend from church, Dean, was calling to inform me he had just played golf with the man I was going to marry. He told me Mr. Wonderful would be at a Bible study on Wednesday and to make sure I was there.

As soon as I walked into the room I spotted him. Yes, Mr. Wonderful was tall, dark, and handsome. After exchanging pleasantries with a few of my friends, I decided to introduce myself. He was very nice but seemed more interested in talking to my friend Helen than to me.

But a couple of weeks later, he called to ask me to dinner. We quickly fell in love. We also fell into temptation.

Click!
A Beautiful Dress, a Beautiful Bouquet, a Broken Heart

This was the day I had dreamed of. I was surrounded by everyone I loved. My dress made me feel like a princess, and the church and reception hall had never looked more beautiful. But as I walked down the aisle, my heart was broken. I pressed my bouquet against my chest hoping no one would see the shame I had buried there. You see, just a few months earlier, I had found out I was pregnant.

I was terrified to tell my friends for fear of being an outcast. *After all,* I thought, *if they find out I'm not perfect, then I can't be a Christian.*

I knew well the sting of rejection and decided to go somewhere I wouldn't be judged. So I went to an abortion clinic and was told the procedure would be quick, easy, and that I'd never think about it again.

The moment I woke up from the anesthesia I knew I'd regret this decision for the rest of my life. The shame and the guilt overwhelmed me.

Now, here I was, walking toward my soon-to-be-husband about to promise to love another when I so desperately hated myself.

Click!
A Little Ray of Hope

Not too long after we returned home from our honeymoon, all the guilt and pain from our mistakes began to haunt us. Our marriage was falling apart. After several counselors seemed unable to help us, one wise, older pastor told us he felt we needed to let God do a work in each of our hearts as individuals, then God would knit our hearts together.

About this time, I started to attend a post-abortion Bible study at the local crisis pregnancy center. There I met a God I'd never known before. According to the Scriptures we studied, He was a loving God who would forgive and who could heal the hurts of His people.

The process was slow and painful, but as I dealt with the abortion, my heart felt hope for the first time.

Then I found out I was pregnant. At first I was overjoyed that God would entrust another baby to me. I had harbored such fears that I'd never be able to get pregnant again. But my joy was overshadowed by my struggling marriage. I knew what it was like to have a mommy and daddy who didn't love each other, and I didn't want that for my child. My husband, Art, and I claimed Jeremiah 29:11, "'For I know the plans I have for you,' declares the LORD, 'plans to prosper you and not to harm you, plans to give you hope and a future'" (NIV).

A few months later we gave birth to a beautiful baby girl whom we appropriately named Hope.

Click!
A Mirror Like No Other

I'll never forget the day I read for the first time a list of Scripture verses that told me who I was in Christ. I read that I was a holy and dearly loved child of God. That He was my heavenly Father. That nothing could separate me from His love. That He sent His Son, Jesus, to die on a cross so I could be forgiven and my slate wiped clean.

Before, when I had looked in the mirror, all I could see was an abused, rejected little girl who had turned her back on God when she couldn't understand Him. Then she had an abortion and thought that was one sin that could never be forgiven.

But that's not what God saw. He saw a child He loved dearly. He longed for fellowship with her. His heart broke over the things that caused her so much pain.

When I finally looked into God's Word and let Him be my mirror, I saw the truth of who I really was for the first time. The chains of bondage started to release their painful grip. John 8:32 says, "You shall know the truth, and the truth shall make you free." The truth is Jesus died to set all people free from hopelessness. I had had a religion but never an ongoing, personal relationship with God.

The day I made those discoveries, I met two people. I met the Jesus I never really knew before. And I met Lysa TerKeurst, a holy and dearly loved child of the most high King, who is accepted and set free.

Click!
The Little Country Church

Soon after I came to understand my identity in Jesus, I was working on a Bible study that asked a difficult question. Would I go and do whatever God asked me to? At first I said, "Yes, of course," and attempted to move on to the next question. Again and again my eyes were drawn back to the first question. God was making me examine more than just the question; I was examining my heart.

You see, I felt God's call to share my testimony, but I wasn't willing. A few weeks later I drove to a little country church where I had a speaking engagement. I told God I would share my testimony just this time.

Tear-stained faces all over the room confirmed that this was a message people needed to hear. More than half the women in attendance recommitted their lives to Christ. As I drove home, I promised God I would go wherever He called me to go and share my story, our story.

Click!
A New Path

Isaiah 61:3 promises that God will "...bestow on [me] a crown of beauty instead of ashes, the oil of gladness instead of mourning, and a garment of praise instead of a spirit of despair" (NIV). It's called amazing grace. He has filled me with His love, and that love now spills over into every area of my life. I'm now able to love my husband, and our marriage is a good one. I'm able to be the kind of mommy my children deserve. My home is a joyful place (most of the time); I'm able to manage my time and money so I can give to others and glorify God. My friendships are characterized by an openness that fosters loving accountability. I can extend my hand to the community with Christ's love. I can do all this not because of myself and my strength but because of God working in me and through me.

I still mess up. (I know all too well that none of us is perfect.) But that's why we need a personal, ongoing relationship with the One who is.

FOUR

Rendezvous with God

SHARON

Do you remember the first time you met your husband? You wanted to know everything about him: what he liked to eat, how many people were in his family, what he was looking for in a wife, his favorite childhood memory, and so on. You wanted to spend every waking hour in his presence just sitting beside him or walking hand in hand through the park. Eventually you knew his innermost thoughts and desires because of the time and effort you put into the relationship.

Our relationship with the Lord is similar. Becoming a Christian is only the first step; for the relationship to become intimate and ongoing we regularly must spend time getting to know our Lord. Just as a strong marriage benefits from having regular date nights, we need to set aside a date with the Lord each day. Using the acrostic DATE, let's look at four simple steps to develop an ongoing relationship with God.

D:
Determine to Set Your Priorities

One of my neighbors has a booming home-based business painting primitive folk art pictures and gift items. Each day as I drive by Susan's house, I notice a small cardboard sign propped against her mailbox. She has an arrangement with the UPS man. If she has an order for him to ship, she sets out a sign that reads, "UPS—Yes." When he sees the notice, he knows to pick up her packages. If she doesn't have an order ready, she puts out a sign that reads, "UPS—No," and he understands that he doesn't need to stop that day.

Sometimes I think we treat the Lord like Susan's UPS man. On days when our burdens seem heavy, when our to-do list has no room left in the margins for one more emergency, we put out a sign that reads, "Jesus Christ—Yes!" because we want His help. But then on the days when life is going well and we seem to have everything pretty much under control, we put out a sign that reads, "Jesus Christ—No," meaning we don't feel we need Him that day. Of course we don't have a literal shingle, but do we have one placed over our hearts? To sustain a relationship with God that's growing in intimacy and maturity, we must determine that every day will be a "yes" day.

In my workroom, I have two identical jars. One is three-fourths full of sand. The other contains fist-sized rocks. The jar of sand represents my activities on any given day: to-do lists, shopping, community projects, painting, cleaning. The list is as…endless as, well…grains of sand. The other jar containing the rocks represents what God wants me to do on any given day: spend time with Him, study His Word, and pray.

If I fill the jar with large rocks first, then, amazingly, I can pour all the sand into the same jar and it fits in nicely around the spaces and crevices. However, if I begin by filling the jar with sand and then try to squeeze the rocks into the same jar, they won't fit.

Likewise, if I start my day spending time with God (the rocks), everything else (the sand) seems to fall into place. If I spring out of bed and hit the floor running to tackle all the tasks that I feel are so necessary for the day, somehow my time with the Lord just never seems to fit in.

Jesus said to Martha, "Martha, Martha, you are worried and bothered about so many things; but only a few things are necessary, really only one, for Mary has chosen the good part, which shall not be taken away from her" (Luke 10:41). Mary started her day with the big rocks. Undoubtedly, Martha started with sand.

I keep these two jars in my workroom to remind me of my priorities. Augustine suggested that we pray for an hour a day. And if it looks as if the day is going to be busy, pray two hours. I know that most of us don't have the luxury of spending two hours with the Lord in prayer each day, but we can determine to spend some.

A:
Appoint a Specific Time Each Day

Remember when you and your husband-to-be were dating and you thought he was the cutest, smartest, funniest, and finest guy you had ever laid eyes on? Remember the chills and thrills on the day he told you he was in love with you and wanted you to be his wife? Well, let's suppose that during his proposal, he promised to be absolutely faithful to you…364 days out of the year. Down on one knee, he holds your hand, gazes into your eyes, and tells you he loves you with almost all his heart, but he does have this thing for blondes and, well, you are a brunette. But he promises to love you almost all the time.

What would your response be? Or should I say, which one of his eyes would you choose to blacken?

31

We never would make a lifetime commitment to someone we felt wasn't committed to us. Jesus wants that same kind of commitment from His bride—complete surrender.

My husband, Steve, graduated from dental school in 1981. One thing that amazed me, in starting a dental practice, was all the emergency phone calls he received on nights and weekends. One night the phone rang at about 2:00 A.M. I groggily picked up the phone and managed a weak, "Hello."

"Hello," the woman on the other end said. "My son is having a terrible toothache. Is the doctor in?"

"Yes, he is," I answered. "Ma'am, how old is your son?"

She answered, "Twenty-seven. My son is twenty-seven years old."

Twenty-seven! I was so shocked I quickly sat up in the bed, accidentally jerking the phone cord out of the wall and disconnecting the caller. She didn't call back.

I had envisioned a distraught mother with a crying five-year-old or maybe a ten-year-old. But twenty-seven!

I lay back down grumbling, "Lord, why is it that people won't go to the doctor regularly but only want help on demand when they have an emergency?"

When I quieted down enough to listen, I heard Him say, "Now you know how I feel."

How many of us go to the Lord for six-month checkups at Christmas and Easter? How many times do we call on Him only when we have an emergency instead of going to Him for regular checkups?

When Jesus taught His disciples to pray, He said "Give us this day our daily bread." David and Nehemiah both sought the Lord "day and night," not just when they were in trouble. God provided manna for the Israelites every morning (except on the Sabbath). When a few Israelites tried to sneak extra food so they wouldn't have to gather God's provision the next day, they found their bowls full of worms the next morning. God wants us to seek Him for our daily—not weekly or biannual—bread.

Imagine going into a five-star restaurant and ordering a multicourse meal. Then, when the waiter arrives with your dinner, you look up and say, "Could you please put that in a to-go bag?"

As absurd as that may seem, that's what many of us do with our time of nourishment with God. We grab a bite on the run in the car, on the subway, sitting in the carpool line. Oh, what we miss by not giving Him the attention He deserves and feasting at His banquet table.

My best time to visit with God is in the morning. However, since Thomas Edison invented the light bulb, we seem to live in a world that has blurred the boundaries of day and night, with people working all night and sleeping all day. Other factors make morning a difficult time to have devotions: a new baby, a passel of children, 5:00 A.M. drive time to work, and so on. The time of day you choose for a quiet time with the Lord isn't what's important. What matters is that you spend time with Him each day.

Studies show that it takes seven weeks of doing something routinely to form a habit. Appoint a specific time each day to spend with the Lord and stick to it for seven weeks. When it becomes a part of your daily routine, you're more likely to continue. And what an incredible habit you've formed!

T:
Take Your Cues from Jesus

In setting my priorities to include a quiet time each day, I decided to see what Jesus did. "And in the early morning, while it was still dark, He arose and went out and departed to a lonely place, and was praying there" (Mark 1:35).

Here we see several facets of Jesus' time with His Father. What did He do? He prayed. When did He do it? In the early morning. Where did He go? Off by Himself. Why did He have a quiet time with God? To talk to His Father and to set His priorities for the day.

Notice that when the disciples looked for Jesus, they always knew where to find Him—praying. Mark 1:36-38 says that while Jesus was praying, Simon and his companions searched for Him, found Him, and said to Him, "Everyone is looking for You." And He replied, "Let us go somewhere else to the towns nearby, in order that I may preach there also; for that is what I came out for." That was His focus for the day. He had received His "marching orders" from God, and He was going to stick to them. Would going back to Capernaum and healing more people have been a good cause? Yes, it would have. But it wasn't what God had planned for that day.

I don't know about you, but by 8:30 in the morning, my phone is ringing with all kinds of requests and demands that threaten to pull me in several directions. But by spending time with God first thing in the morning, I'm able to set my priorities and say yes or no with confidence. When we take our cues from Jesus and start our day meeting with God, it helps us keep our focus on what He has called us to do and not on what everyone else wants us to do.

Some of the greatest moments in a Christian's life are a result of spending time in prayer. Jesus spent all night in prayer before He chose His disciples (Luke 6:12). He defeated Satan's temptations after praying and fasting for forty days (Matthew 4:3-11). Prayer preceded His miracles (John 11:42-43) and gave Him the strength to go to the cross (Luke 22:39-42).

The disciples observed Jesus' prayer life and asked Him to teach them to pray as He did (Luke 11:1-4). He told them seven simple steps (Matthew 6:9-13).

      "Our Father who art in heaven." Acknowledge
        you are a child of God and He is your almighty

Father.

   "Hallowed be Thy name." Praise God for who He is and for the holiness of His name and character.

   "Thy kingdom come, Thy will be done on earth as it is in heaven." Pray for His will to be done in your life and the lives of those for whom you intercede. Praying the Word of God is praying the will of God.

   "Give us this day our daily bread." Pray daily for your needs.

   "And forgive us our debts, as we also have forgiven our debtors." Pray for God to forgive you, as being in His presence will bring conviction of sin. Also, give your grudges to God and forgive those who have offended you.

   "And do not lead us into temptation, but deliver us from evil." Pray for protection from the world, the flesh, and the devil.

   "For Thine is the kingdom, and the power, and the glory forever. Amen." God is the eternal King of kings, whose rule knows no end. He is omnipotent, omniscient, and omnipresent. Amen.

Did the disciples take their cue from Jesus and learn how to pray? Yes, they did! In Acts 2, during their prayer time, the Holy Spirit descended on the disciples and gave them power to spread the gospel throughout the world.

In *Experiencing God,* Henry Blackaby writes, "Prayer is not a substitute for hard work. It is the work!"[1] Prayer isn't meant to change God's mind. It's supposed to change us and to align our thinking with God's.

E:
Equip Yourself for Every Good Work

You run out to your mailbox and discover four envelopes: a bill from the power company, a flyer from a department store, a note from Aunt Betty, and a letter from God. Now, which one would you open first? I don't know about you, but I'd open the letter from God. And the truth is we face that choice every day. God has written us a wonderful love letter, full of incredible treasures, words of endearment, and instructions to equip us for life. All we have to do is open the pages of our Bibles.

Second Timothy 3:16 says, "All Scripture is inspired by God and profitable for teaching, for reproof, for correction, for training in righteousness; that the man of God may be adequate, equipped for every good work." First Peter 1:13 says, "Therefore, gird your minds for action."

I love the picture of dressing my mind for action. When I'm going through stressful times, my dreams portray me as someone whose mind isn't dressed for action. I tend to have three recurring dreams. In one I'm in high school. It's the day of final exams, but I realize I haven't gone to that class all year. In my second dream, I'm working as a dental hygienist with one patient in the chair and five patients in the waiting room. I'm two hours behind and can't find my instruments. In my third dream, I'm standing behind a podium in a crowded room. I'm not dressed in a power suit but in my birthday suit. After some consideration, I realized that each of these nightmares is about not being equipped—not being prepared.

In Matthew 25:1-13, Jesus tells about five ladies who were prepared and five who weren't. The Jewish custom was for a bridegroom to come in the middle of the night, surprise the bride and her bridesmaids, and whisk them away to the wedding celebration. Their duty was to be ready at all times. It seems that five of the ten ladies in this particular group were "fired up," so to speak. They had plenty of oil in their lamps and were well equipped. However, the other five weren't prepared. At the last minute, they rushed out to do a little shopping to buy some more oil.

But wouldn't you know it, Jesus—I mean the bridegroom—came while the ill-prepared gals were out at the mall. When they came back, their prepared friends were long gone to the celebration with the bridegroom.

Oswald Chambers says, "A ready person never has to get ready." As we commit to have a rendezvous with God on a regular basis, we will become intimate with Him and know His ways. We will be equipped and ready for whatever life brings our way.

An old saying suggests that, after many years of living together, married couples start to look alike. As the bride of Christ, after many years of spending time with God, others will notice that the two of you bear a striking resemblance to each other.

Broken Dates and No Shows

Perhaps as you've read these pages, you've thought, *I remember when I gave my heart to Jesus, but that seems like eons ago. Since then, I've drifted away from Him.* Perhaps the embers of your first love are smoldering. Do you desire to rekindle the flame?

Oh, He thought you'd never ask. "Return to Me," declares the Lord of hosts, "that I may return to you" (Zechariah 1:3).

I remember when I learned how to snow ski. The first thing the instructor said was, "Lie down in the snow. I'm going to teach you how to get up."

I thought that was a strange way to begin to learn how to ski. However, I soon saw the instructor's wisdom, because the first thing I did was fall.

In our ongoing relationship with the Lord, we all will fall at times. We all will make mistakes. If you're discouraged because you've fallen or turned your back on the Lord, know that you are in good company.

One of the greatest heroes in the New Testament, Peter, also turned his back on Jesus, right during His time of greatest need. Peter denied he even knew who Jesus was. After the resurrection, Jesus pulled Peter aside. He didn't criticize, reprimand, or humiliate Peter. Jesus didn't even tell him to try harder next time. Instead, He simply asked Peter to reaffirm his love. Three times Jesus asked, "Peter, do you love me?"

That's what He's asking you. "Daughter, do you love Me?"

Even though we may break dates with God and occasionally not show up when He's waiting to have fellowship with us, His love never changes. "Draw near to God and He will draw near to you" (James 4:8). He says, "Call to Me, and I will answer you, and I will tell you great and mighty things, which you do not know" (Jeremiah 33:3).

He's waiting. Will you join Him?

FIVE

Up Close and Personal

SHARON

I grew up in an upper-middle-class neighborhood in eastern North Carolina. Our home was a traditional brick ranch-style with columns supporting the front porch and sixty-foot pine trees forming a shady canopy over our roof. The azaleas and immaculate lawn portrayed the picture of tranquility and peace, but inside the walls teemed an atmosphere of hostility and fear.

My father was a successful businessman who was gone most of the time. When he was home, he had bouts of heavy drinking, and my parents fought, both verbally and physically, in my presence. Black eyes, broken furniture, and heated arguments were common occurrences. I remember going to bed at night, pulling the covers tightly around my chin, and praying that I would hurry and fall asleep to shut out the noise of the screaming and shouting. I felt that I lived on an earthquake fault line; I never knew when the "big one" was going to hit.

Amazingly, my family went to church on Sundays and heard politically correct, ear-tickling sermons. The messages were moral enough to make us feel we had "done our American duty" and light enough not to offend us.

Dutifully, I joined the church after a six-week confirmation class and was baptized to "seal the deal." But, as the pastor took me under the water and raised me up "to newness of life," as he stated, I was no more a new creation than John Doe buried in the local cemetery. I was more concerned with my hair getting messed up in the water than with my eternal soul. The following Sunday, I walked across the stage in my crisp, white dress and received a pin and certificate to commemorate the occasion. It was official: I now had religion.

"But God"…I think those are the two most beautiful words in Scripture. But God wasn't finished with me yet.

When I was thirteen, the mother of a friend of mine took a special interest in me. The Hendersons lived two blocks from our house, and Wanda, their redheaded daughter, and I began to spend a lot of time together. I loved being in their home. Mr. and Mrs. Henderson hugged and kissed in front of us and even called each other pet names. For the first time I saw what a relationship between a husband and wife was supposed to be like. In my adolescent mind, I didn't understand why their home was so different from mine, but I knew that difference had something to do with Jesus Christ.

The Hendersons loved church. That was new to me. I'd never known anyone who loved church. As far as I knew, church was just something nice families did. You went to the dentist twice a year, had your tires rotated every 10,000 miles, paid your light bill once a month, and went to church on Sundays.

But it didn't take me long to realize the Hendersons didn't love church, they loved Jesus, whom they celebrated at church.

Eventually, the Hendersons invited me to attend church with them. Because a really cute boy was in the youth choir, I went. Then Mrs. Henderson started a Bible study for the teens in the neighborhood. I attended and soaked up every word she had to say.

At times, I thought Wanda's mom was a little kooky—what with all this singing praise choruses and talking about Jesus as if she knew Him personally. But I was drawn to the light that shone in her.

One summer evening, Wanda invited me to spend the night at her house. Sitting on the couch in the den, her mom asked me, "Sharon, are you ready to accept Jesus as your personal Savior and make Him Lord of your life?"

Even though I wasn't sure how all that was possible, with tears streaming down my cheeks, I said, "Yes, I'm ready."

The three of us held hands and prayed the prayer that changed my life. I finally understood the words from a verse I had memorized when I was a little girl, "Arise, shine, for your light has come" (Isaiah 60:1). The light had come into my life and driven the darkness away. Jesus is that light, and as Scripture says, "He delivered us from the domain of darkness, and transferred us to the kingdom of His beloved Son" (Colossians 1:13). Now I had more than a religion; I had a relationship.

As wonderful as that night was, I knew I couldn't stay at the Hendersons' house forever. I had to go back home. But one thing was for sure, Jesus was going with me. He began the process of filling me with His love so I could spill over to my family. My group of Christian friends prayed that God would intervene and draw my parents to Himself.

My mom and dad thought I had gone off the deep end with this whole "religion thing" but at the same time were somewhat relieved that "it" would keep me out of trouble. Still, the fighting and the drinking continued. But now a different kind of fighting was occurring simultaneously—a spiritual battle for my parents' souls.

Whenever your life is filled with Christ, it will inevitably spill over to those around you. Whether you are a neighbor reaching out to a hurting child, a counselor volunteering in the community, or a youth worker coming alongside a struggling teen, splashes of His love will touch those whom God puts in your path.

In this case, I lived out my faith in front of my parents. Oh, I got in trouble from time to time, talked disrespectfully, broke curfew, and struggled with authority. I was still a teenager, after all. But I also loved Christ more than anything on earth. That total abandonment, coupled with a teen's energy, is hard to ignore.

Two years after I accepted Christ, I had the opportunity to study abroad. Immediately, I rejected the idea.

"Who will take care of my parents?" I asked my friends. "Who will break up the fights?"

I hadn't learned that God wants to carry all my burdens. I knew that He wanted to answer my prayers, but I had trouble believing He didn't need my help.

I prayed with my friends and a group of adult mentors and decided I should go to Europe for the summer. I packed my bags, prayed for Jesus' shed blood to protect my home, and flew across the ocean.

My first night away, my dad came home drunk and angry that my mom had allowed me to leave the country. I had told my mom to go to Mrs. Henderson's if she needed anything. As Dad's rage escalated, Mom ran to the haven two blocks away. That night, God answered a young girl's prayer, and my mother gave her life to Jesus Christ. The light had come to her life as well.

She went back home and told my dad what had happened. "Allan," she said, "I just want you to know that I love you no matter what, and I forgive you for all the things you've done."

The change in my mom had a dramatic effect on my dad. At the end of the summer, I came home to a new family. I've always joked that God had to get me out of the country so He could get the job done, but there's probably a bit of truth in that.

We continued to pray for my dad. He always had said, "Sharon, I've done some bad things in my life, some things that I don't think God could ever forgive. I'll keep trying to be good, and maybe one day I'll be good enough, but not right now."

"Dad," I answered, "you'll never be good enough. If we could be good enough, if we could earn our way to heaven by doing good works, then Jesus would have never had to come and give His life for us. He knows that we can't do it, so He did it for us."

But God's depth of grace, mercy, and love was too unfathomable for Dad to grasp.

Three years later, after a business deal had gone terribly awry, he was on the verge of a nervous breakdown. It seemed to him that his world was spinning out of control. At the end of his rope, he found himself sitting on a log in the woods of Pennsylvania, pouring his heart out to a pastor who was doing construction work on his church.

"Sharon," my dad later said to me, "I told this man everything I had ever done. He said that he had done some of the same things himself before he was a Christian—and this guy was a preacher! So I figured if God could forgive him, He could forgive me too. The pastor told me all I had to do was to confess that I was a sinner, ask God to forgive me, confess Jesus as Lord, and believe in my heart that God raised Him from the dead, and I would be saved."

"Well, Dad," I said, "what did you do?"

"I prayed with that man. I gave my life to Jesus."

In a matter of five years, God had showered me with His abundant love, and His goodness had spilled over to my family. But the story doesn't end there.

As a matter of fact, it never ends. Just as Leviticus, Numbers, and Deuteronomy include the long lists of so-and-so begat so-and-so, God uses us to beget other spiritual children. You may not be able to list the people who have benefited from God's power flowing through you, but splashes of His presence are all around.

All of the other six principles depend on the first. Without a personal relationship with Christ, our well would be dry. We would have little to nothing to give to others around us. Please remember, this isn't about having more religion in your life. You can be "religious" about many things: church, exercise, diet, and so forth. All through the Gospels of Matthew, Mark, Luke, and John, God shows us religious leaders who were some of the most miserable men of their day. Jesus, on the other hand, chose twelve men with whom to have a relationship, and through them He changed the world. Likewise, He can use you to change yours.

SIX

Being Emptied
of Yourself

LYSA

*I*f a want ad were written for what I do, it would sound something like this:

> *Wanted: Wife to a loving husband and mother to six children. Also would work with a growing ministry to women. Qualifications: Must come from an intact family in which a good marriage was modeled. Must have had a loving father so she will have a healthy self-image and solid parenting modeled from which to draw wisdom in raising children. Needs to have walked the straight and narrow so she can be a good example to other women.*

Well, I certainly wouldn't qualify for the life I have today. As a matter of fact, if I'd seen this ad when I was single, I never would have applied. Thank goodness God doesn't work as we do. He picks unlikely candidates for jobs all the time.

Just look at Moses the murderer. He grew up as an adopted son in Pharaoh's house. He had power, prestige, and wealth. Yet one moment of anger led him to murder, and he lost it all—or did he? After spending forty years wandering in the desert, Moses, sent by God, traveled back to Pharaoh's house to lead the Israelites out of captivity.

Take a gander at David the adulterer. In one moment of lust for another man's wife, he forsakes his own marriage and commitments to God. He then plots to have this woman's husband killed. Yet David was called a man after God's own heart.

We mustn't forget about Rahab the harlot. Now, if I were God, I don't think I would let any of my male servants close to a woman of Rahab's chosen profession. But while I would only look at the circumstances of her life, God saw this woman's heart. Rahab hid the Israelite spies in her home, and in turn God protected her family and allowed them to live with the Israelite people. And Rahab became a great-great-multiplied-times-great grandmother of Jesus Himself.

So what are God's qualifications to be used by Him and to have an up close, personal relationship with Him? I think there's just one. "Man looks at the outward appearance, but the LORD looks at the heart" (1 Samuel 16:7). God is looking for devoted hearts, repentant hearts, hearts that are willing to be emptied of self and filled with Him. When a person is willing to let God work on his or her heart, God will make that individual into a new creation. Moses became a leader, David a man after God's own heart, and Rahab forgiven and redeemed.

If you could have talked to these individuals in the middle of their history-making ventures, I'm certain you would have heard them use words like "scared," "unsure," "doubtful," "under-qualified," "unable," "unworthy," and "incapable."

Aren't you glad God doesn't see things as we do? He didn't see these people as powerful creatures capable of accomplishing great things on their own; He saw them as flawed individuals with hearts willing to have His power flow through them.

Maybe you experience some of those same insecure feelings about the call God has placed on your life. Well, please know that what God did to change those people, He can do for you—and He has done for me too.

Before I could overflow with God's love into other people's lives, I had to be emptied of many things—bitterness, anger, resentment, feelings of worthlessness and rejection. I had to forgive my abuser and allow God to be my avenger. I had to forgive my father and realize that terrible things must have happened to him to cause him to act toward me as he did. After all, as I was once told, "Hurt people hurt people." I wanted the cycle to end with me.

I also had to be emptied of my questions to God: "Why me?" "How could You have let this happen?" Now, when I share my story with women's groups, I see how God is working all these things together for good. So many women have come to trust Jesus as their Savior because they catch glimpses of His love and grace through my testimony.

And secrets of impurity and poor decisions had to be unlocked and released to God's grace. Then, instead of focusing on what I had lost, I could turn my focus to what God had allowed me to gain, including compassion for others who had made mistakes, a desire to help others, and a deeper walk with my Savior.

Yes, I was abused as a child. Yes, I had a father who rejected and abandoned me. Yes, my heart broke over the loss of my dear sister. Yes, I was angry and rejected God for a time. Yes, I fell into sexual sin and aborted an innocent child. Yes, I was filled with regret, shame, anger, and bitterness. But God emptied me of all this, held me up high, and proclaimed, "This is My holy and dearly loved child. I do not condemn her and neither will you, Satan. She is now set free from your chains of bondage, and I will use her for My glory."

All of heaven rejoices when one of God's own is emptied and set free. But I must tell you that the party doesn't last long. Satan will try to use your past as ammunition against you. You see, being emptied of self is a continual process. Sin, self-centeredness, and past insecurities can creep into your heart in an instant. That's why it's vitally important to daily walk with God and to ask Him to search your heart and to reveal any wicked or untrue ways within.

Psalm 139:23-24 says, "Search me, O God, and know my heart; try me and know my anxious thoughts; and see if there be any hurtful way in me, and lead me in the everlasting way." If you are willing to pray this Scripture, then you are well on your way to being emptied of self. The most beautiful part of this verse is the assurance that being emptied of self means being led in the everlasting way. And, ultimately, the everlasting way is a pool of water that overflows with God's love, spilling onto others around you.

That's why a personal, ongoing relationship with Jesus Christ is Principle #1 for the Proverbs 31 woman. If your relationship with Jesus is stagnant, then you can't possibly overflow with His love into the other areas of your life.

Remember the example of the seven waterfalls? Let's walk to the edge of that first pool. Stick your toes in and feel the water. Peek over the edge of the waterfall to see what's spilling over into the other pools…your relationship with your husband, your children, your home, your time and money, your friends, and your community. As your life spills over into each of those areas, is it evident that Jesus is the Lord of your life? That you've been emptied of your past hurts so you can be filled with God's love? Is there enough water in the first pool to continue the waterfall all the way to the bottom?

Let's take a plunge into the second pool now to consider how our marriages can be richer because we've been to the refreshing source of God Himself through reading His Word, praying, and spending time alone with Him.

Splashes from John

SHARON

*I*n the Bible, water is used to portray the cleansing, filling, and healing power of God's Word. Many times Jesus' ministry took place in or around water. Amazingly, water is mentioned in the first seven chapters of the Gospel of John, with each chapter having a direct correlation to one of the seven principles in this book.

Before moving from one pool to the next, let's stop, sit by the water's edge, and dip our toes and hearts into the refreshing water of God's Word.

John 1

In the first section of this book, we've focused on the first principle: The Proverbs 31 woman reveres Jesus Christ as Lord of her life and pursues a personal and ongoing relationship with Him. In John 1, the Gospel writer places his focus there as well. He actually takes us back to another first recorded in the first chapter of Genesis: "In the beginning was the Word, and the Word was with God, and the Word was God" (John 1:1).

When we look at Genesis 1, where do find Jesus? We find Him "moving over the surface of the waters" (verse 2). Even in the beginning of time, Jesus had a strong connection with water.

Just as we've established the need to know Jesus Christ before we can flow into the other areas of our lives, John also establishes that we need to know Him. Verses 1-18 are like an overture to a symphony of Scripture. An overture in a symphony acts as a teaser, making the listener eager to hear more of the theme music as it's played throughout the presentation. John's explanation of who Jesus is sets the tone for the entire book. The first eighteen verses of John 1 stir my heart to want to know more about the Messiah, the Anointed One, God made flesh, who existed before the creation of the world and now gives life and light to men.

Later in the opening chapter of the Gospel of John, we come face-to-face with Jesus at the Jordan River in Bethany. His cousin, John the Baptist, was a remarkable young preacher who drew great crowds with a message of repentance and preparation for the Messiah's coming. He baptized believers as an outward symbol of their inward confession and repentance. Even though Jesus needed neither because He was the sinless Son of God, John baptized Him in the Jordan as an act of obedience—Jesus obeying His Father and John the Baptist obeying His Messiah. Jesus' emergence from the water signaled the beginning of His public ministry.

Baptism symbolizes identification with someone or something. Baptizing a person "in the name of" someone (Acts 8:16) indicates that the baptized person is closely bound to or becomes the property of the one in whose name he is baptized.[1]

As we sit by the first pool, we have to ask ourselves a few questions.

Have I identified myself with Jesus Christ?

❧ Is my heart bound to His?

❧ Have I given myself over to His lordship in my life?

If you haven't, I pray you will get up from the water's edge and stand under the first waterfall. Ask Jesus to save you, fill you, and use you. Let His love rain down on you, cleanse you, and make you new. Here's a prayer to help express your heart:

> Dear Lord, I confess that I'm a sinner and that sin has separated me from You. I thank You for sending Your Son, Jesus Christ, as a sacrifice for my sin. I'm asking now that Jesus Christ reside in my heart and become the Lord of my life. Your Word promises that if I confess with my mouth that Jesus Christ is Lord and believe in my heart that You raised Him from the dead, I will be saved. Thank You, God, for saving me and making me Your child. Amen.

If you prayed that prayer, you are now a child of God. Welcome to the family!

And God said, "I will make rivers flow on barren heights, and springs within the valleys. I will turn the desert into pools of water, and the parched ground into springs" (Isaiah 41:18 NIV).

Love, Honor, and Respect Your Husband

SEVEN

Marriage: Frustrating or Fulfilling

LYSA

*P*rinciple 2: The Proverbs 31 woman loves, honors, and respects her husband as the leader of the home.

My husband, Art, met Sabrina shortly after he and I returned from our honeymoon. Sabrina made her way into our home and almost sent my husband over the edge. She's loud, always wants the last word in an argument, and loves to hold a grudge. Her husband goes to the city gates to escape her rather than to sing her praises. The funny thing about her is that she looks just like I do, except she wears a scowl instead of a smile. OK, OK, she is me, the Proverbs 31 woman in her not-so-finest hour.

I tell you about Sabrina because I want you to know that I don't have this marriage thing all figured out, and, yes, I too have days when I'm ready to call it quits.

I've seen both sides of marriage, the frustration and the fulfillment. My husband and I have been in the pit of marital despair when we thought our relationship was a life sentence of doom and gloom. I've also known what it's like to simply drift in marriage, when we operated more like business partners, coexisting and sharing responsibilities, but were devoid of the romantic spark that keeps a relationship alive and growing. I also know what it's like to enjoy the wonder and fulfillment of a growing marriage.

No matter what kind of marriage you have, you fall somewhere on the continuum between isolation and oneness. Every marriage will grow either toward the oneness God intended when He created marriage or toward the bitter isolation that sometimes ends in divorce.

Many people view marriage as an automobile. They are so excited when they first buy their new car that they won't even let anyone eat or drink in it. They keep it serviced and cleaned, and they drive it carefully. Then time passes, and all kinds of fast-food wrappers are scattered within, the oil should have been changed two thousand miles ago, and what's one more little scratch or dent since they're trading in the old thing soon anyway.

In the same way, marriage can get a little old and lose the excitement that first drew a couple together. At that point, some people think, *I deserve someone better. Time to trade him in on a newer model.* In light of how easily a marriage can slip away from the dream we began with, what can we do to protect and preserve our marriages?

Read on. We are at the second pool's edge, ready to wade through the waters. Won't you take time to check the water to make sure it's pure and clean? Let's filter our marriages though God's Word and make sure they're all the Creator intended them to be. Let's check the reflection that's being mirrored. Are we reflecting God's love? Are we being the wives God intended? The kind our husbands can stand at the city gates and praise? Are we glorifying God in the way we fulfill our roles as wives? Well, let's step in and discover how to become the wife our leader, lover, and friend needs us to be.

EIGHT

Leader:
The Gift Only
a Wife Can Give

SHARON

*S*everal years ago, Steve and I decided to take ballroom dance classes. I had seen couples gliding across shiny dance floors, moving as one to the fluid sounds of a melodious orchestra. That's what I wanted to do. I wanted us to be Fred Astaire and Ginger Rogers.

We signed up for our six dance lessons, but instead of gliding around the room we learned to make boxes with our feet. I quickly became bored with the "slow, slow, quick, quick" march and asked the instructor if we could move around the room a bit. So she taught us how to make a box with its lid open: two steps sideways and two steps forward.

Actually, Steve moved forward; I had to move backward. This seemed unfair to me. Why did I have to be the one to move backward? Now, I understand that we can't both move forward. We would be on a collision course for certain. But why me?

The instructor assured me that this was the way God had planned it and told me to stop complaining. (She didn't say it exactly like that, but that's what she meant.)

After a few dance classes, I didn't look like Ginger Rogers; actually, I resembled Fred Rogers. Nor were we flowing around the room, moving as one. It was more like Steve was pushing a shopping buggy around the room.

I use the word "push" because I wasn't guided easily. More than once, the teacher tapped me on the shoulder and said, "Mrs. Jaynes, you're leading again."

It can be difficult at times to let our husbands be the leaders of the home; however, that's what God created them to be. And when we follow God's plan for marriage, whether we understand it or not, we have a greater chance of living happily ever after.

Now, before you get in a huff, thinking this material is archaic, listen to what Anabel Gillham, author of *The Confident Woman,* has to say,

> You may be thinking, *This is the twenty-first century, not the Dark Ages! Woman has come a long way since your day, Anabel*. You're right; it is archaic. In fact, I'm going back to the first century for my material, checking with the One who made the machine. He designed it. He knows how it works most effectively. Archaic or not, the failure of one out of every two marriages proves that our twenty-first century program isn't working too well. We're doing something wrong. We're making some big mistakes, and one of them is usurping the husband's role as leader.[1]

Since this material originated in the garden, let's look at God's original intent. In Genesis 1, God created light, the heavens, waters, land, plants, sun, moon, and animals. Then on the sixth day He created "man in His own image" (Genesis 1:27). All that He made was good except for one thing. He said, "It is not good for the man to be alone; I will make him a helper [completer] suitable for him" (Genesis 2:18).

Now, before you get in another "snit fit," as Patsy Clairmont calls it, let me remind you of some significant others who share the title "helper." David prayed, "O Lord, be Thou my helper" (Psalm 30:10b). Jesus, talking about the Holy Spirit, said, "I will ask the Father, and He will give you another Helper, that He may be with you forever" (John 14:16). So I'd say we're in pretty good company.

Yes, God had special plans for woman, but being the leader of the home wasn't one of them. He is a God of order, and two heads always has been considered a deformity. His plan is stated plainly in 1 Corinthians 11:3, "But I want you to understand that Christ is the head of every man, and the man is the head of a woman, and God is the head of Christ."

Yes, as far as our culture is concerned, we've come a long way, baby, but it's not looking too good. Our culture has been on a downward spiral in matters of the home, particularly when it comes to a husband's role as leader. We see this every day on television. Over the past fifty years "dads have taken a drubbing, being demoted from patriarch and pillar to, in the words of 'Home Improvement's' Jill Taylor, 'pathetic.'"[2] Television shows of the fifties and sixties, such as *Leave It to Beaver, Make Room for Daddy,* and *Father Knows Best,* portrayed dads as a wellspring of wisdom, compassion, and guidance.

By the end of the sixties, that began to change. *All in the Family* featured Archie Bunker, a bigoted, bungling oppressor. Then came Tim Taylor of *Home Improvement* with the recurring theme of Tim messing something up and his wife, Jill, straightening it out. I could go on with *the Simpsons, Roseanne,* and the *Berenstain Bears.* But suffice it to say, fathers on TV no longer help family members overcome obstacles; instead dads are portrayed as creating or even becoming the obstacle.[3] If any other segment of society were berated in such a way, the public would protest.

What are we doing to our men? Society is slowly stripping them of the role God intended for them from the beginning.

Let me share with you part of a letter I received from one of our ministry's radio listeners.

Dear Proverbs 31:

I heard your radio show last week while I was on the road, and while I do not listen to this type of show normally, I somehow felt compelled to listen this time....My wife and I have been married for seven years. These days not much is going on between us, and some of it has to do with huge differences of opinions. When we married, I was looking for a "partner," that is, someone to complement me in the areas that I am not so good in and to help me in life....The general lack of respect that she has for my leadership of the household has tremendously reduced any level of intimacy that we share....It is as if we are just two people living together, and I want a marriage. I want someone whom I can trust with my feelings, without being betrayed. I want someone who places me #1 in her life. I want to be important to my wife. I want her to respect me. I don't want to force these things on her....

This listener goes on to say that his wife is a very nice person. He simply longs to be the leader of the home and to have her become a true partner. At least twenty to twenty-five percent of the calls our ministry (which was created to encourage women) receives are from men who long to have the kind of relationship with their wives we talk about in Proverbs 31 Ministries.

Consider these words from Ephesians 5:33: "And let the wife see that she respects and reverences her husband—that she notices him, regards him, honors him, prefers him, venerates and esteems him; and that she defers to him, praises him, and loves and admires him exceedingly" (AMP). In the words of Scarlett O'Hara, "My, how you do go on."

Let's look at the directives in this verse and their opposites to see how we stack up.

Do We		Do We
Respect	*or*	Show contempt
Reverence	*or*	Dishonor
Notice	*or*	Ignore
Regard	*or*	Disregard
Honor	*or*	Humiliate
Prefer	*or*	Exclude
Venerate	*or*	Belittle
Esteem	*or*	Mock
Defer	*or*	Usurp
Praise	*or*	Criticize
Love	*or*	Hate
Admire	*or*	Ridicule

Why do we women struggle so with the issue of leadership? I think it goes back to the garden. We've already established that God created us as unique and special, but man was given the role of leader. Note that just a few verses after God made Eve, she's already taking the lead, disobeying God, and dragging a rather weak Adam along. Because of Adam and Eve's disobedience, each received several curses from God. One of the curses or judgments placed on Eve was "your desire shall be for your husband, and he shall rule over you" (Genesis 3:16b).

Some commentators say this verse refers to sexual desire. But my husband would say, "That's not a curse! That's a blessing!" I think it means that woman will desire to rule over man. And she's been trying to rule over him ever since. The idea of man ruling over woman has been a thorny issue ever since, too.

One day I was preparing for a radio interview with a station that owns 150 networks (smaller stations) all around the world. That means the interview would be aired at the same time in many different areas. We were going to talk about the seven principles of Proverbs 31 Ministries. I offered to send the announcer some interview questions ahead of time, but he said, "No, thanks. I have a few of my own." Major red flag.

With trepidation, I went to the radio studio for the interview. "Welcome to our program today," he began. "Joining me in the studio is Sharon Jaynes of Proverbs 31 Ministries, and our topic is submission."

Hey, wait a minute, buddy. That's not our topic. It's the seven principles, I thought. Of course we were on the air so I just smiled.

Submission. It's such a touchy subject. Perhaps if the interviewer had told me the topic ahead of time, I wouldn't have been so eager to join him. Thankfully, after about five minutes on the subject, he moved on. However, he needed a "hook" to reel in the audience, and the subject of submission was certainly an attention-getter.

Actually, all Christians are called to a life of submission. Ephesians 5:21 says, "Submit to one another" (NIV). Scripture tells us to set aside our selfish desires and to serve one another. And husbands are called to servant leadership. "Husbands, love your wives, just as Christ also loved the church and gave Himself up for her; that He might sanctify her, having cleansed her by the washing of water with the word...So husbands ought also to love their own wives as their own bodies" (Ephesians 5:25, 26, 28a).

The word *submission* comes from a combination of words that mean "to arrange under."[4] Even though we are to submit one to another, God is a God of order, and He has set up the following chain of command in the home: wives submit to husbands, who submit to Jesus, who submits to God. That doesn't mean the husband is a dictator and the wife is a doormat. Remember, Ephesians 5:25 tells the husband to love his wife as Christ loved the church and gave His life for her. That doesn't sound like any dictator I've ever known. It sounds like sacrificial love.

Bryan Chapell, writer for *World* magazine notes, "Biblical leadership involves sacrificing one's self for the sake of another. A biblically guided husband looks past his own right to consider what's right for his spouse. Following Christ's example, such a husband refuses to abdicate the responsibility of leadership for the family, but uses his biblical authority to arrange the family's resources and activities to serve the best interests of his wife and children."[5]

Submission doesn't mean a wife can't offer advice and wise counsel. The Proverbs 31 woman did just that in verse 26, "She opens her mouth in wisdom, and the teaching of kindness is on her tongue." It doesn't mean she walks around saying, "Yes, dear. Whatever you say, dear."

But it does mean, when the husband and wife don't agree on a decision, the wife defers to the husband's wishes. "But what if I know I'm right?" you might ask. To obey God is the "ultimate right." After all, we're accountable to God for our obedience.

When it comes to submission, we have three choices:

- Lovingly submit to our husbands and support them in their leadership.

- Begrudgingly submit to our husbands, complete with pouting, sulking, cold shoulders, nonverbal hostility, and a bounty of "I told you so's" if their decisions turn out unfavorably.

- Refusing to submit, thereby winning the battle but chipping away at the foundation of the marriage.

I've done all three. Number one is best. A few times, my bad attitude toward submitting was so unbearable that Steve, against his better judgment, gave in to my wishes. Did I feel victorious for getting my way? Maybe for about twenty seconds, until I realized I was robbing my husband of his

God-given role as leader of the home and disobeying my heavenly Father. I was Eve all over again!

During my radio interview, the interviewer asked me a common question: "What about the wife who is married to an unbelieving husband? Does she need to submit to him?"

"Dave," I answered, "if we have a president who isn't a Christian, do we still submit to him? Of course we do."

But we aren't just left to draw parallels. Peter tells us, "Wives, in the same way, be submissive to your husbands so that, if any of them do not believe the word they may be won without words by the behavior of their wives" (1 Peter 3:1 NIV). Loving submission to an unbelieving husband preaches a sweeter sermon than our words ever could.

Exceptions do exist to following your husband's leadership: if he asks you to do something illegal or contrary to the Word of God. In that situation, go to your pastor for wise counsel.

Sheldon Vanauken, in his book *Under the Mercy,* tells about four women who made an incredible discovery about the results of submission. These four women met for a weekly Bible study and came across the passage in 1 Corinthians 11:3 about the husband being the head of the wife. The women were faced with a decision.

> The leader for that evening read the verse aloud, paused and read it again....Every one of those women—they all knew it—was head in her marriage.

> Someone said weakly, "Does St. Paul say anything else about [headship and submission]?" An index was consulted, and the other Pauline statements (Col. 3:18; Eph. 5:22; 1 Tim. 2:11) were read out. There was some discussion. Finally the leader said, "Well, girls, what do we do?" Someone else said, "We've got to do it."

Then came the miracle. In less than a year the four women, with amazement and delight, were telling each other and every other woman they knew what had happened. The husbands, all four, had quietly taken over…and, with no exceptions, every one of the women felt her marriage had come to a new depth of happiness—a joy—that it had never had before. A rightness.

Seeing this astonishing thing that not one of them had thought possible…the four wives one day realized an astonishing further truth: They realized that their husbands had never demanded and would never have demanded the headship; it could only be a free gift from wife to husband.[6]

Well said, Mr. Vanauken.

Not only is the husband the leader in the relationship, but he also is the wife's lover. As is the case with leadership, the wife can offer "gifts" that go a long way toward helping her husband be the kind of lover she always dreamed of. Read on to learn more.

NINE

Lover:
Romance Revisited

LYSA

*M*ost of us, before we were married, dreamed of long, passionate lovemaking with our husband-to-be. You know the romantic dream I'm talking about. Your bed was draped with gauzy white material. You and this man of your dreams were lovingly caressing each other while beautiful music played and candlelight danced among the room's shadows.

Now let's fast forward to reality. Somewhere between dirty diapers, monthly bills, laundry, little Suzy getting scared and climbing into bed with you, and waiting up for your teenager to return home from a date, the romantic dream has long since been forgotten. Maybe you now dream of being able to go to bed without anyone touching you.

Well, take heart; you're not alone. Many women struggle with keeping their sexual desire alive. Now, I know for some of you this isn't a struggle, but read on; there's still some good information here for you.

I surveyed more than a thousand women for my book *Capture His Heart,* and I found out, not surprisingly, that sex was on the minds of many women. I received more comments, quotes, and suggestions on sex than on any other topic. Two of the most talked about aspects of sex were the frequency of intercourse and the desire to be romanced. Let's see how these two actually go hand in hand.

In *Intimate Issues,* authors Linda Dillow and Lorraine Pintus tell of a scene from a movie in which a husband and wife each talk with a therapist. On the left half of a split screen, the man complains, "We hardly ever have sex. Maybe three times a week, tops." On the right half of the screen the woman laments, "We are constantly having sex. We must have it three times a week!"[1]

This dialogue is consistent with the age-old tension that exists between many husbands and wives. One night my husband and I were having this "frequency" discussion. I was trying to paint a word picture to help him understand that, just because I didn't want to make love at times didn't mean I didn't love him. I explained that as a mother of young children I'm on touch overload by the time I go to bed. It's as if I was very full, and someone placed my favorite dish in front of me and told me to eat up and enjoy. While I might really love this particular meal, I'm simply too full to partake.

Art listened intently. Then he painted his own version of this word picture. In his version, he hadn't had anything to eat in several days and was close to being famished. Then someone placed his favorite meal in front of him but instructed him he must only look, not touch or partake.

So how can we resolve this and enjoy God's gift of sexual intimacy? Romance has a lot to do with it. You see, to continue my word picture, a wife needs to be made hungry again. Most women will only long to be touched sexually if they feel filled emotionally.

But not all husbands are naturally romantic. Since we can't change our husbands or control what they may or may not be willing to do, let's talk about the things we can change. I think we can do three things to fill up emotionally and to rekindle our sexual appetite.

Romance 101:
Rekindle Your First Love First

I wish I could say I was a virgin when I got married, but you know from reading my testimony that I wasn't. You also know about the sexual abuse and rejection I faced before most kids even know those things exist. All of these negative experiences had a negative effect on the way I approached my marriage bed. Old tapes of bad past experiences would play in my head and interrupt the tenderness between Art and me.

Maybe you too faced situations similar to mine, and sex has become a dirty word. Let me encourage you to take these feelings to God. Let Him heal you and give you a new view of sexual intimacy. Isaiah 43:18-19 says, "Do not call to mind the former things, or ponder things of the past. Behold, I will do something new, now it will spring forth; will you not be aware of it? I will even make a roadway in the wilderness, rivers in the desert." In this verse God reveals His mercy to Israel despite His people's unfaithfulness.

God can make a way for us to forget the things of the past and experience the sweet intimacy He intends for sexual relations with our husbands. For me, when I rekindled my love with God and sought to understand what the Scriptures tell us about sex, my desire to be sexually intimate with my husband was rekindled.

God's Word tells us that sex is incredible. Genesis 4:1 in the King James Version tells us that it allows a husband and wife to "know" each other. The Hebrew word referred to in this passage as "know" means to know sexually. This kind of intimate knowledge between a husband and a wife is more than just a physical knowledge. It connects two people physically, emotionally, and spiritually. Genesis 2:24 says, "A man shall leave his father and his mother, and shall cleave to his wife; and they shall become one flesh." This is a beautiful picture of two becoming one in the most intimate of ways in God's eyes. God doesn't refer to sex as bringing a couple close or even connected. He refers to it as becoming one.

Beautiful benefits come from this oneness. It creates life and amazing pleasure.

I remember being awed when each of our children was born. Our love created three of the most beautiful blessings I've ever seen. Out of our love, God allowed a part of Art and a part of me to join Him in creating life. What an amazing thing! God made our bodies to fit together just right and for each to contain half of what is needed for life to be created.

Making love can also provide intense and wonderful pleasure. Let your desire be only for the amazing man God has given you as your husband. Think of all his qualities that made you more attracted to him than any other. Remember the thoughts you had of him when you were dating. Song of Songs 2:3-4 says, "Like an apple tree among the trees of the forest, so is my beloved among the young men. In his shade I took great delight and sat down, and his fruit was sweet to my taste." Song of Songs 4:9-10 goes on to say, "You have stolen my heart, my sister, my bride; you have stolen my heart with one glance of your eyes, with one jewel of your necklace. How delightful is your love, my sister, my bride! How much more pleasing is your love than wine, and the fragrance of your perfume than any spice!" (NIV). Intoxicate your husband with the sweet pleasure only you can provide him and at the same time allow yourself the wonderful experiences of sexual arousal and pleasure.

If you struggle with feeling pleasure during lovemaking, pray and ask God to help you enjoy this experience as He intends. Also, I recommend reading Linda Dillow and Lorraine Pintus' book, *Intimate Issues,* published by Water-Brook Press.

By rekindling your love for God and His Word and seeking His perfect design for sexual intimacy, your marriage bed can become more fulfilling than ever.

Romance 201:
Find Time for Yourself

Bob and Rosemary Barnes, in their book *Great Sexpectations,* talk about the importance of having enough energy to make love and the difference in sexual energy levels for men and women. They say,

> A woman goes through life with one large battery that gives her energy. This battery gives her the energy to do all things. This battery energizes her to work, to relate, and to have sex with her spouse. When the battery is run down, she finds it difficult to do anything. A man, on the other hand, has a battery that energizes everything he does, except sex. He can be totally exhausted, with this main battery run down to zero power. Then he gets into bed and a second little side pack battery kicks in! This little extra battery powers nothing but his sex drive. No matter how tired he may be, if the side pack gets triggered, he's in business.[2]

Finding time for yourself enables you to have both the desire and the energy to make love. Keeping myself physically fit does more for my sexual desire than almost anything else. When I exercise, I feel better about my body and better about letting my husband touch me. Interestingly, sex therapist Dr. Linda DeVillars noted that twenty-seven percent of women report an increase in their ability to climax after beginning an exercise program.[3]

After my first child was born, I weighed nearly two hundred pounds. I hated my body and could hardly stand to let Art touch me. When I set aside time for myself, started exercising and taking better care of myself, I felt more attractive and willing to be vulnerable. Since I need to feel somewhat sexy to be sexually intimate, little things like painting my nails, getting my hair cut, and putting on perfume help me to feel attractive and to have the desire to attract my man.

If you have small children or a really hectic schedule, set aside time for yourself. Remember that your relationship with your husband is a top priority, second only to your relationship with God. If taking time for yourself will enhance your relationship with your husband, then write it into your schedule and make it a priority. This isn't selfish; it's a wise investment!

Share this need with your husband and ask him how he could help to give you this time. I guarantee if he knows your having time for yourself will enhance your sex life, he's a lot more likely to help you find the time.

Speaking of time, timing is everything when it comes to making love. Take time for a quick nap during the day or tell your husband you would love to romance him tonight and suggest you go to bed early enough to still have the energy to do so. If you're too tired at night, suggest to your husband that the two of you plan romantic times in the morning or on weekend afternoons.

Romance 301:
Find Time for You and Your Husband

It's no big secret that men and women are created differently. When it comes to sex and romance, that is especially true. Men are visually stimulated while women are emotionally stimulated. Whenever I do a marriage seminar, I bring two ads that I found in the same women's magazine. The first is a shoe ad that captures a man's ideal picture of a woman. The ad uses few words but shows a woman dressed in a pink silky slip and high heels. She is happily cleaning a toilet with a sensual expression on her face. Now, please don't think I'm bashing men here. God made them to be visually stimulated, and I guarantee if your husband came home and saw you dressed like this woman with the same look on your face, he wouldn't care what you were cleaning. He would whisk you off to bed.

The second ad is for a Lane cedar chest. It pictures a husband and wife in a tender embrace, and their story is written out. Supposedly she saves everything he's ever given her, and now he's bought her a special cedar chest to put it all in. How romantic and emotionally stimulating! When a husband does something that thoughtful and sweet, a woman can't help but be attracted to him.

But how do we bridge the gap between a husband's desires and a wife's desires? I believe the answer lies in good, honest communication. Most women, including me, make the mistake of assuming our husbands are mind readers. But your hubby can't possibly meet your expectations if he doesn't know what they are.

The kind of communication I'm talking about requires time in which the two of you can be alone and feel safe to share your expectations with one another. If you don't feel you can express your true feelings orally, write them out before you sit down with your spouse and read your letter aloud. The most important thing is for each of you to share what's on your heart about your intimate relationship. As you think about what you want to express, pray about your expectations to make sure they are fair and realistic. Then ask your husband to do the same.

Next, find some time to be alone and have a heart-to-heart talk. If you have small children, trade babysitting with another family or ask a family member to help you out by watching your children. Ideally, get away for a couple of days to some-place where you can spend long, restful days in conversation and private evenings of romance and love. Make it fun by helping each other create a list of things you can do for each other to show your love and commitment. This time together will be rewarding and a wise investment.

Remember, you will only get as much out of your romantic relationship with your husband as you put into it. Too many people make the mistake of thinking this intimacy stuff should come naturally. While it is natural and wonderful, just like everything else that's inherently great, it's even better if you work at it.

Determine to walk through the stages of romance we've discussed with a new desire for your husband. God designed intimacy for two people to get lost in sweet love and amazing passion. So grab that man of yours and suggest you steal away and get lost for a while.

TEN

Friend: Creating Commonalities

SHARON

I remember sitting in front of a mirror on my wedding day, brushing my hair, and musing about the joy and love I felt for my bridegroom. Then I thought, *Doesn't every bride feel this way about her groom on her wedding day? What causes fifty percent of marriages to end in divorce? What could possibly mar this beautiful union?* Staring at myself in the mirror, I made a commitment never to let the following words pass my lips: "We just grew apart." "I don't know him anymore." "There's no spark between us." "We don't have anything in common."

I became an avid student of the key ingredients of a successful marriage. In the eighties, few books were written on the subject, but I remember one book that stirred my heart. *A Severe Mercy,* by Sheldon Vanauken, was an autobiography of love between Sheldon and his wife, Davy. It wasn't meant to be an instructional book, but it held many treasures.

One of the gold nuggets I discovered in its pages was:

"Look," we said, "what is it that draws two people into closeness and love? Of course there's the mystery of physical attraction, but beyond that it's the things they share. We both love strawberries and ships and collies and poems and all beauty, and all those things bind us together. Those sharings just happened to be; but what we must do now is share everything. If one of us likes anything, there must be something to like in it—and the other one must find it—every single thing that either of us likes. That way we shall create a thousand strands, great and small, that will link us together. Then we shall be so close that it would be impossible—unthinkable—for either of us to suppose that we could ever recreate such closeness with anyone else. And our trust in each other will not only be based on love and loyalty, but on the fact of a thousand sharings—a thousand strands twisted into something unbreakable."[1]

The media remind us how opposites attract. *Men Are from Mars, Women Are from Venus* was on the best-seller list for months. Yes, men and women are different, and praise the Lord for that, but our society has lost what it means to "become one." Many hear the words "and the two shall become one," but they just can't decide which one. When couples extinguish the two candles in the wedding ceremony after lighting the unity candle, they too often begin a journey of continuing to snuff each other out. "A thousand sharings" is where unity is created.

Commonalities in Work

My husband is a dentist, and I have a degree in dental hygiene. I worked with him to build his practice and to understand what he does all day. I can sympathize with the struggles of getting the PFM margin on the facial of #8 just right. Lysa's husband owns a Chick-fil-A franchise, and she goes into the restaurant occasionally to help.

I know it's rare for husbands and wives to share the same profession, and most of the time counselors recommend they not work together. But I do encourage you to learn about what your husband does at work. Is he a stockbroker? Take a class at a local community college and learn to read those little numbers in the *Wall Street Journal.* Is your husband a banker? Learn about IRAs, mutual funds, and compound interest. Is your husband a builder? Go to the construction sites and watch his progress. Learn about Sheetrock quality or why a 2 x 4 is really a $1\frac{1}{2}$ x $3\frac{1}{2}$. Is he a salesman? Know his product.

Could one reason a man has an affair with a woman at the office be because she has entered into his world? I encourage you to enter your husband's world and to show interest in what he does, not just the paycheck he brings home.

Commonalities in Play

Sharing commonalities applies to outside interests as well as interest in his work. Willard Harley, in his book *His Needs, Her Needs,* notes that one of a man's five greatest needs in a wife is recreational companionship.[2] While your husband might not express this desire to you, he longs for your company in play.

Does he like football? Learn what a tight end does and why the official keeps throwing those handkerchiefs in the air. Does he play golf? Learn why a birdie is better than a bogey. Does he like to hunt? Learn how to cook venison. Does he read *Sports Illustrated*? Pick one up every now and then and browse through the pages. He'll be amazed at your "wisdom."

Lysa's husband loves to exercise. While this was never her forte, sharing this with Art has been one of those thousand sharings that ties them together.

Now, don't get me wrong. You can't share every activity with your mate. Steve took one look at my golf swing and said, "Honey, why don't we just take some ballroom dance classes, and you let me stick to the golf." That was fine with me.

The following actions create commonalities and communicate that you enjoy your husband's company and that he belongs to you:

- Plan times when just the two of you can be together.

- Ask to be with him, to go to the store or run an errand with him just so you can enjoy his company. "If you'll wait five minutes, I'll go with you."

- Take him to a weekend getaway, just the two of you, and buy some pretty, flimsy lingerie for a nice surprise.

- Tell him, "I like it when you go shopping with me." "It's fun to drive around together."

- Go for ice cream, a picnic in the park, a scenic drive, a boat ride, people-watching at the mall, a walk around the block, fishing, boating, hunting, biking, a baseball game, a football game, a rodeo, a car museum, a train museum, a plane museum, an antique mall, a planetarium, a science-fiction movie, working in the garage, walking the dog, etc.

These simple suggestions speak volumes of love to your husband.

Commonalities in Goals

Before the Industrial Revolution, husbands and wives shared common goals. My paternal grandparents owned and operated the Middlesex General Store. My maternal grandparents ran a farm with the help of their twelve children. I doubt they ever sat down and mapped out their hopes and dreams, because working for common goals was a way of life.

But this isn't the agricultural age. Husbands and wives are going in a million different directions, and if we desire to remain unified, we must be intentional and set common goals. In our home, Steve and I share financial goals, spiritual goals, ministry goals, giving goals, and parenting goals. Each year, we evaluate our progress and make adjustments.

Bob and Rosemary Barnes, in their book *Rock-Solid Marriage,* note, "Setting goals is only the beginning. If you don't establish a way of reaching your goals, then it's really only a dream; a goal is a direction you decide to go in. A dream is something you just wish would happen, but you don't do anything about it. Dreams fade away if they don't become tangible goals. If you don't have goals, you go through life working hard, but never feeling like you're getting anywhere."[3]

You know how excited and fulfilled you feel when you put those big check marks on your to-do list. Imagine how thrilled you would be to reach goals of much more significance.

If you desire to become one with your mate, you will want to create commonalities. When you do, you will be doing more than sharing his interests; you will be sharing his life.

No "His" and "Hers" towels hang at our house. We're living out one life in two bodies. As Sheldon Vanauken said, "And our trust in each other will not only be based on love and loyalty, but on the fact of a thousand sharings—a thousand strands twisted into something unbreakable."

Significant Others

Of course, a couple of challenges arise in creating these commonalities. Among the most common problems in marriages today, three top the list: sex, money, and in-laws. While we hear the words "What God has joined together, let no man put asunder," sometimes the couple's own families seem to be the ones doing the "asundering."

An ample supply of mother-in-law jokes floats around these days, but in-law problems are no laughing matter. As I've searched the Scripture, I've found very little on how to handle the situation. However, one verse does resound: Genesis 2:24, "For this cause a man shall leave his father and his mother, and shall cleave to his wife; and they shall become one flesh."

Steve and I have always felt the number one priority in family is our family. Before we had children, it was our family of two. When Steven Jr. was born, it was our family of three. This decision has made both sets of in-laws angry when we didn't meet expectations, especially during the holidays. However, it has kept our little family unified.

Couples face several in-law problems. How often do we visit? How long do we stay? How long do the in-laws stay when they come to visit? Where do we spend Christmas or Thanksgiving? Do we spend vacation time with in-laws? How much do we tell our in-laws about our personal finances? Our marital struggles? Our parenting decisions?

Questions like these can be difficult to agree on. But the most important point is to reach an agreement before the problem stares you in the face (or knocks on the door), causing marital discord. Remember, the most important family unit God has ordained is your spouse and you.

God does, of course, call us to honor our fathers and mothers. We aren't to ignore them or their needs. But He also calls us to leave them and cleave to the mate that He has chosen for us. Dr. James Dobson, in his book *Solid Answers,* states, "If either the husband or wife has not been fully emancipated from the parents, it is best not to live near them. Autonomy is difficult for some mothers and fathers to grant, and close proximity is built for trouble."[4]

Do your in-laws help you to build a godly home that lasts a lifetime? Or are they out-laws who rob you of the oneness you committed to on your wedding day? Pray about it. Talk about it. And above all, enjoy the miracle of two becoming one.

Another big challenge a couple faces is when two become three. Family psychologist Dr. John Roseman noted, "Today's typical wife, as soon as she becomes a parent, begins to act as if she took a marriage vow that read, 'I take you to be my husband, until children do us part.'"[5]

I can remember a time, and not too long ago, when a wife who became a mother remained first and foremost a wife. A woman who worked outside the home was referred to as a "working wife." The woman who worked in the home was referred to as a "housewife."

But a paradigm shift has occurred in our way of thinking, and the verbiage we use. Today's woman in the same circumstances is referred to as a "working mom" or a "stay-at-home mom." Some may think that this is a change for the better; after all, who wants to be married to her house? But I see a grave problem. Our focus has shifted from a home that is centered on the marriage unit to one that is centered on the children.

Roseman goes on to say, "This shift came about largely because as America shifted to a self-esteem based child-rearing philosophy, women became persuaded that the mother who paid the most attention to and did the most for her child was the best mom of them all."[6]

Unfortunately, many times this has occurred at the expense of the marriage. The wife becomes engrossed in her children's lives, and the husband becomes engrossed in his career. Twenty years later they look up from their cereal bowls and say, "Who are you?"

I believe that the best mom of all is one who loves her husband and gives her children the security of living within the protection of a rock-solid marriage, a marriage that exemplifies and models for them what God intended.

So guard your marriage from in-law and child-oriented diversions. Be your husband's friend and draw the two of you closer through commonalities in work, play, and goals. Soon you'll find that a thousand strands bind you together in a fulfilling marriage.

ELEVEN

Making Your Marriage Last

LYSA

A newspaper on the West Coast ran this ad: "Wedding Rings for Annual Lease."[1] I guess this company decided to capitalize on the growing market of those who enter into marriage with an escape clause.

This escape mentality is a deception straight from the Devil. You see, Satan knows if he can deceive us into breaking the covenant we made before God to love, honor, respect, and cherish our spouse, then he has a foothold to destroy our relationship with God. That's because marriage is the physical representation of a beautiful spiritual truth: Christ is called our Bridegroom and the church His beloved bride. To distort our view of earthly marriage is to shake our relationship with God to its core.

Am I overspiritualizing? I don't think so. Wrapped up in this connection between our earthly bridegroom and our heavenly Bridegroom rest three components that can help a marriage last: Pursuing an intimate relationship with God, pursuing an intimate relationship with your spouse, and pursuing healthy acceptance of yourself.

Pursuing an Intimate Relationship with God

At the beginning of my marriage, I was constantly frustrated by my husband's inability to meet my needs. I criticized him for not making me feel loved, wanted, and needed. I thought the problem was with him, and I was diligent in my high and mighty prayer sessions instructing God how He needed to fix this man of mine. Then one day God broke through my self-centered attitude and pierced my heart with a significant, life-changing truth: God never intended my husband to meet all my needs.

For my husband to even try this impossible task would be dishonoring to God. Oh, God does require my husband to love, honor, respect, and take care of me, but never does God's Word say a man should meet his wife's every need.

Instead, God has placed within all of us a void only He can satisfy. When I finally understood what it meant to pursue my own intimate relationship with the Lover of my soul, my relationship with my husband changed. I stopped demanding that Art change and started to pray that God would change me. I took my focus off what I felt were my husband's weaknesses and inadequacies and started to focus on submitting to God's call for my life. The more time I spent seeking Jesus and allowing Him to fill me with His incredible love, the more I was transformed into the wife my husband needed and deserved.

I'm my husband's bride for a short time on earth. Together we will build a life, raise precious children, dream about our future, and laugh as we grow old and wrinkled. But one day I will hear the call of my heavenly Bridegroom. Because I have allowed Him to woo me and because I have listened to His voice many times, I will know His call and will follow Him to the great wedding in which He will take my hand in an eternal marriage. Only then will I be complete, full, whole, and holy.

We should try to be the best wives we can to our husbands because that honors God. However, our husbands also have needs that only God can meet. If your husband has made mistakes and has sought to have his needs met outside of your marriage and His relationship with God, he will need to answer to God. I would encourage you to pray for him and to ask God to direct your path.

Pursuing an Intimate Relationship with Your Spouse

I love the quote "The day you said, 'I do,' you chose your love; since then you have been learning to love your choice." Learning to love your choice is an important component to a thriving marriage.

"Marriages Made to Last," an article in *Psychology Today*, includes a listing of the top answers men and women gave to the question, "What keeps a marriage going?" The men responded:

- My spouse is my best friend.

- I like my spouse as a person.

- Marriage is a long-term commitment.

- Marriage is sacred.

- We agree on aims and goals.

- My spouse has grown more interesting.

- I want the relationship to succeed.

- An enduring marriage is important to social stability.

- We laugh together.

- I am proud of my spouse's achievements.
- We agree on a philosophy of life.
- We agree about our sex life.
- We agree on how and how often to show affection.
- I confide in my spouse.
- We share outside hobbies and interests.[2]

I love any information that helps us women peek inside men's hearts and minds. Some common threads seem to run through the male gender, even though guys come in all shapes and sizes and vary as much as women do. To pursue an intimate relationship with our husbands, it helps to take a look at this list and use it to open up the lines of communication. Ask your husband what he thinks makes a marriage successful. If he has a hard time coming up with his own answers, show him the list and ask him to circle the answers he most agrees with. Spend some time on your next date talking about ways to get to know each other more intimately and to make your marriage last.

I also would encourage you to pull out from this section the practical suggestions we've given to help you love your husband as leader, lover, and friend. Take time to invest your energies in your marriage.

Marriage is like that great toy you received on Christmas morning. You could hardly wait to rip open the package and start playing. However, someone forgot to read the small print on the package's front. "Batteries not included." No batteries, no fun. The same is true with marriage. It has the potential to be great fun if we're willing to invest the necessary energy. We have to make the effort to really get to know each other—our likes and dislikes, our turn-ons and turnoffs, our dreams and fears. Only then will our marriages be the intimate expressions of love we desire.

A Healthy Acceptance of Yourself

I remember standing at the altar on my wedding day wondering whether or not I really could love Art as I was promising. I wasn't sure I could love someone else when I didn't even like myself. I don't think this view is uncommon for women. At one time or another we've all struggled with our identity and self-worth. It wasn't until I understood my identity in Christ that my whole perspective changed.

When I finally saw myself as a dearly loved child of God, I could then see my husband as a dearly loved child of God as well. Placing this kind of value on both of us opened my eyes to the way God sees us. God looks at us through the shed blood of His Son and sees us as forgiven and holy. It must break His heart for us to see ourselves as anything less than fearfully and wonderfully made.

So what does this have to do with a great marriage? Genesis 2:25 says the man and woman were "both naked and were not ashamed." They felt perfectly comfortable with who they were, and they knew they were accepted by the other. It wasn't until Satan slithered onto the scene in chapter 3 that they sinned, felt ashamed, and made fig leaf clothing to cover themselves. And we've been trying to cover ourselves ever since.

Let me encourage you to stop covering whatever is drawing you away from your true identity in Christ. Spend time with God in prayer and in His Word. Ask Him to give you a new view of who you are in Him. By loving yourself, you will be able to love your husband more fully.

Pursuing an intimate relationship with God, pursuing an intimate relationship with your spouse, and pursuing a healthy acceptance of yourself all make major contributions to a marriage that will last—and that will satisfy both of you.

TWELVE

For As Long As We Both Shall Live

SHARON

*O*ne of my favorite fictitious characters is Uncle Billy Watson in Jan Karon's Mitford series. Uncle Billy was an elderly man married to Rose, an eccentric schizophrenic. Rose was often seen parading around town in her deceased brother's combat boots and a bomber jacket or in a chenille robe, argyle socks, and a shower cap. But for forty-three years, through all her escapades, Uncle Billy remained faithful. One day, the leading character in the series, Father Kavanaugh, commented, "Uncle Billy, I don't know how you've lasted with Miss Rose all these years." "Well, I give 'er my word, don't you know."[1]

"I give 'er my word." I made a promise. It sounds so simple. But somehow we've made a mockery of the words, "till death do us part," and marriage has become another toss-away in our throw-away society.

Unfortunately, thanks to Hollywood, our generation has an unrealistic view of love. Romance in the movies isn't real life. Lovers on film don't have bad breath, flat tires, or nausea. Nor do they wait three hours in line at the Department of Motor Vehicles, cut grass, wash dishes, take out the garbage, or scrub toilets. People fantasize about relationships like the ones they see on TV.

Then Satan whispers in your ear, "Of course you don't have a romance like they have, but you could. All you have to do is find the right person. Right now you're stuck with the wrong guy."

So what's the answer? Stay committed to your husband and make it work. Don't even think about Plan B. Someone asked Ruth Graham, wife of evangelist Billy Graham, if she had ever considered divorce. She replied, "Divorce, no. Murder, yes."

Commitment Through the Storms

On May 11, 1987, a precious friend of mine, Elizabeth Patten Brafford, came into the world. She was a fragile 6 lbs., 2 oz., redheaded angel with delicate features, cherub lips, and far-set eyes characteristic of children with Down syndrome. She was a flicker of light to all those around her, especially to her parents, Bill and Alice. Her fragile heart had a hole that couldn't be repaired and irregularly pumped blood through her body. Little Elizabeth was in and out of the hospital for five months before God decided she had fought long enough. On October 24, He took her in His arms and ushered her to a new home in heaven, where she waits to be joined by her mommy, daddy, and four siblings.

While fifty percent of all marriages end in divorce, the statistics jump to a staggering seventy percent when a child dies or is born with a deformity.[2] Elizabeth's mom, Alice, was no stranger to hospitals. She is an oncology nurse and knew these statistics all too well.

"As tragic as losing Elizabeth was," Alice told me one day, "I knew the greater tragedy would be losing our family."

Unfortunately, most couples have no strategy for handling the storms of life. They don't think past the romance of the honeymoon. Then, when a storm hits, they panic or run in opposite directions.

Several years ago, Hurricane Hugo swept through our town and left it looking like a war zone: roads blocked with toppled sixty-foot trees, downed power lines jumped wildly in the streets, and homes cut into pieces. We knew the storm was coming so we had time to prepare as best we could, stocking up on water, flashlights, and canned goods.

Alice compared losing Elizabeth to going through an emotional hurricane. She and I talked about how couples could prepare for the storms and stay committed to the course. Here's what we came up with:

- Secure your home. Secure your family to the solid rock of Jesus Christ.

- Practice emergency drills. Discuss the "what ifs" before they happen. The week before Elizabeth was born, Alice asked, "Bill, what would we do if something was wrong with this baby?" He answered, "We'll handle whatever comes, and we'll handle it together."

- Protect your valuables—your relationship with each other.

- Make it a community effort. After Hurricane Hugo, whoever had a grill shared it with anyone who needed to cook, and neighbors' chainsaws buzzed for weeks cutting up toppled trees. In a crisis situation, allow your church family and friends to help you through.

- Gather your supplies. Be grounded in the Word of God.

- Huddle in the center of your house. During a crisis, pull together instead of drifting apart.

After the storm has passed, communicate your feelings and commit to stay together, no matter what.

Bill and Alice are heroes to me. They weathered the storm and now help other couples through their losses and grief.

Commitment Through the Desert

Everyone loves a good love story. Boy meets girl. Boy pursues girl. Girl marries boy. They ride off into the sunset with the words "and they lived happily ever after" rolling across the screen.

If we could listen in on their conversation as they glided toward the sunset, we would be shocked to hear something like this:

"Honey, this has been a glorious day," the bride chirps. "Now let's give this marriage our best effort for about three years. Then I'll start feeling taken for granted and act grumpy and moody."

"That sounds reasonable," he chimes in. "Then after a few years of your unpredictable moodiness, I'll start spending more time at the office and maybe even start seeing another woman. You won't mind because by then you'll be disenchanted with me anyway. How's that?"

"I guess that's OK. Then I'll pour my whole life into the kids and have periods of depression."

As absurd as this sounds, it's exactly what happens time and time again.

Dr. John Cuber, in his book *The Significant Americans,* notes that one or two out of ten couples will achieve "intimacy" in a relationship.[3] By intimacy, he was referring to the process of two separate individuals melding together to become "one flesh."

Perhaps more wearing on a marriage than the inevitable storms of life are the desert routines, the mundaneness of every day, and the doldrums of ho-hum-ness. Some days you won't particularly like your husband. Those are the days you tire of his unpleasant habits and feel emotional blandness. The key word is "feel." You may feel despondency at times, but a marriage isn't based on feelings; it's based on commitment. And when you resolve to stay committed, many times the feelings will follow.

I married my husband because I loved him. Now I love my husband because I married him.

Renewing Your Commitment

My friends Chris and Gina divorced after eleven years of marriage. Then Gina attended a wedding, and she listened closely to the vows. "I, Susan, take you, Ted, to be my lawful wedded husband, to love, honor, and obey, in sickness and in health, for richer or for poorer, for as long as we both shall live." The words echoed in Gina's head as she realized she had repeated those same vows not only to her husband but also to God, and she had broken that promise.

A few months later, Gina and Chris decided to remarry and to renew their commitment to each other. As the couple stood in a church gazebo with their three children, the pastor spoke the traditional words in the service. "The ring is an outward symbol of an inward commitment. It is in the shape of a circle that is everlasting and has no end."

"Wait a minute," their eight-year-old son, Jordan, interrupted. "Does that mean Mommy and Daddy aren't ever going to get a divorce again?"

"That's right, son. That's what it means," the pastor replied.

Satisfied with the pastor's answer, Jordan said, "OK, I was just checking. Go ahead."

And so should we all "just check." Are we prepared to commit ourselves to our marriages through the storms and the deserts?

Principle 2 is the second waterfall for a reason. We can't be the wives God intended without His help. We can only begin to be the wife in Proverbs 31 when we have a personal and ongoing relationship with Jesus Christ. The power of the Holy Spirit gets us through the storms and the deserts in this union.

Before leaving the second pool, linger for just a few minutes more. Look at your reflection in the water. Do you see a woman committed to her marriage? A woman who supports her husband as leader of the home, who is his lover and his friend for life? Is she a woman committed to keeping the covenant she made with God on her wedding day? Reflect on that for a while and then ask God to fill you with a deeper love for your husband than you've ever experienced before.

Splashes from John

Sharon

*A*s we sit by the second pool, our thoughts turn to the second principle: The Proverbs 31 woman loves, honors, and respects her husband as leader of the home.

John 2 also turns our attention to marriage, as the writer tells us about Jesus' first miracle—at a wedding reception in the town of Cana. Jesus, His family, and His disciples were invited to the wedding and the gala that followed. Apparently Jesus was comfortable at such parties. I imagine Him laughing, mingling, and having a good time with His friends. Near the end of the festivities, the servants let Mary in on a dilemma—they were out of wine. To run out of wine at a wedding celebration was an embarrassment to the hosting family. Mary turned to her Son and said, "They have no more wine" (verse 3 NIV), as if she expected Him to do something about it.

Jesus answered, "Dear woman, why do you involve me?...My time has not yet come" (verse 4 NIV).

With confidence, she tells the servants, "Do whatever he tells you" (verse 5 NIV). Another translation says, "Whatever He says to you, do it" (NASB). Oh, how I admire a woman who is confident in the power of Jesus Christ! Mary seemed to understand it before anyone else.

As we think about this scene, I want to ask you a question. Did Jesus need the servants' help?

He could just as easily have made the wine miraculously appear without their help. But Jesus chose, just as He continues to choose today, to allow His servants to join Him in His work. He allows us to participate in His ministry and gives us the opportunity to be blessed when we obey.

Jesus told the servants to fill the six water pots with water, and they did so "to the brim." As we serve the Lord, we should follow their example and do it "to the brim"—one hundred percent. In turn, He takes our simple efforts and turns them into something much better.

He is in the transformation business: sadness into gladness, sinners into saints, and miseries into ministries. The most important transformation that occurs in us is when we accept Jesus Christ and make Him Lord of our lives. "Therefore if any man is in Christ, he is a new creature; the old things passed away; behold, new things have come" (2 Corinthians 5:17).

The second most important transformation that occurs in a person's life is when that individual marries and the two "become one flesh." If you haven't been transformed by your marriage, you and your spouse probably live on different planets. Marriage changes us. When we let Jesus work miracles in our marriage, He will take something good and make it better. But just as He desired the servants' participation, He desires ours. He wants us to fill our marriages "to the brim"—to give our unions all we have. And as Mary said, "Whatever He says to you, do it," even if it doesn't make sense to you.

Oh, you can fill the pots a little bit, if that's all you want to give God to work with. Or you can fill them to the brim and let Him work in a mighty way. Then, when the years pass and you grow old with the husband of your youth, you can say with the headwaiter at the wedding in Cana, "You have saved the best till now" (verse 10b NIV).

Nurture
Your
Children

THIRTEEN

True Treasure

LYSA

*P*rinciple 3: The Proverbs 31 woman nurtures her children and believes that motherhood is a high calling with the responsibility of shaping and molding the children who will one day define who we are as a community and a nation.

The day was cloudy and rainy and showed no deference to our plans to play with the children on the beach. After one too many hours cooped up in a small condo with six energized kids, my friend Becky and I knew we needed to get creative. The answer? A treasure hunt complete with a map in a bottle, a buried treasure, and *X* marks the spot.

As soon as the rain tapered off, the hunt began. Six unsuspecting kids ran toward the surf eager to look for shells and crabs.

Then Hope and Ashley spotted the bottle, and the beach was transformed into a scene from a pirate movie. The map, complete with burned edges, led the children up and down the dunes, around the umbrellas and chairs, peeking under beach towels and blankets. Then they discovered a wonderful and helpful surprise. Arrows in the sand pointed out the way, under the boardwalk. We warned the treasure hunters to watch out for offshore pirate ships (that resembled shrimp boats) as the kids scampered under the boardwalk and discovered an *X*. You've never seen little sand shovels dig so fast.

Finally, a silver box was pulled from the sand. It was filled with gold-wrapped chocolate bars and lots of precious, plastic jewels. The kids ran to share their treats with the others on the beach who had witnessed the hunt. The treasure was safe. We were never discovered by the pirates, although later that night our sleepy little treasure hunters made sure we hid the special box before we went to bed, just in case.

As I tucked my jewel-laden children in bed, I thanked God for the rain because it led to such a fun and memorable day. I thought about how raising children is much like a treasure hunt. The treasure we're in search of, however, is so much more significant than gold and jewels. We're hunting for ways to raise kids who know, love, and desire to follow the Lord...an eternal treasure.

FOURTEEN

Jewels, Pirates, and Arrows in the Sand

LYSA

One day my eldest daughter, Hope, came home from school concerned about some mysterious writing that marred her friend's paper. Hope told me she and her friends tried all day to figure out who might have done this. She scratched her head and in a very serious tone said, "Mom, I really thought it might have been the hand of God, but the handwriting was just too messy."

Oh, how her story tickled my heart. Though she is young, she already recognizes that the hand of God is real and present in her life.

In looking for the right way to raise children, the best treasure to give your child is the Word of the living God. This treasure will lead your child's heart straight to the most important decision to be made—to know Jesus and to share His love with others.

Jewels

Ephesians 3:14-21 provides wonderful help for leading our children to love God. Verses 14 and 15 say, "For this reason, I bow my knees before the Father, from whom every family in heaven and on earth derives its name." Here we find a valuable gold nugget. Our children must come to know for themselves that God is our heavenly Father from whom we draw our identity. We are called children of God because through Jesus' death and resurrection we've been saved, redeemed, forgiven, and adopted into the royal family. Talk with your children about what it means to be children of God. Tell them the wonderful riches of our eternal inheritance. Share with them what it means to you personally to be saved, forgiven, and adopted as a child of God.

Verses 16 and 17 offer this help: "[I pray] that [God] would grant you, according to the riches of His glory, to be strengthened with power through His Spirit in the inner man; so that Christ may dwell in your hearts through faith; and that you, being rooted and grounded in love..." A mother can give no more glorious riches to her child than her prayers. Tell your children that you pray for them and ask them to share specific requests with you. Pray these verses for your children, that God may strengthen them with His power so that Christ always would dwell in their hearts through faith. Insert their names into the verses.

Teach your children how to be rooted in their faith and established in love. To be rooted means to be firmly planted. Help them to understand how to stand firm in their beliefs. Explain that roots are also the place from which a tree draws its nourishment to live. Ask them where we draw our spiritual nourishment from and help them to understand what it means to drink the living water of Christ.

Finally, teach them about Christ's amazing love. Share stories from your own life of times Jesus revealed Himself and His love to you. Explain that, as you have come to know Him intimately, His love for you is the solid foundation on which your life is established.

Verses 18 and 19 provide us with these insights: "[You] may be able to comprehend with all the saints what is the breadth and length and height and depth, and to know the love of Christ which surpasses knowledge, that you may be filled up to all the fullness of God." We'll call these gems our red rubies, as they symbolize Jesus' death and resurrection. Explain to your child what Jesus accomplished on the cross. Tell your child that a soldier nailed Jesus' hands and feet to that cross, but His love for your child kept Jesus there. Assure your child that nothing he or she has done or ever will do is too much for God to forgive. Pray for your child that he or she will never seek to be filled with anything of this world but only with the fullness of God.

Verses 20 and 21 reveal other gems: "Now to Him who is able to do exceeding abundantly beyond all that we ask or think, according to the power that works within us, to Him be the glory in the church and in Christ Jesus to all generations forever and ever. Amen." This is the diamond...the pure, sparkling power of Christ in us. We can't even dream or imagine all that Christ has in store for our children. As long as His power is allowed to work in them, amazing things are ahead.

You know we parents—myself included—become caught up in report cards and progress reports to determine how our children will do in the future. While those are important, we must remember what's most important. If our children receive spiritual A's, then we parents can take great comfort in knowing that Christ will do the rest. He has promised all of us in Jeremiah 29:11 a future and a hope, which is better than any dream we might dare to come up with for our kids!

I've just given you a small glimpse inside this wonderful treasure chest of the Word of God. Do you see what comfort and direction it gives? We know that all Scripture is from God. We also know that God knows our children more intimately than we ever will. He was there when your children were formed in the womb. He knows the number of hairs on your children's heads. Shouldn't we trust Him to provide us direction for placing jewels in our children's hearts?

The Pirates

Any seasoned treasure hunter knows that, where treasure is to be found, pirates are waiting in the wings to steal that which is precious. As mothers, we need always to be on alert for that which seeks to steal, kill, and destroy. Our most obvious enemy is Satan, who desires to keep our children from coming to a saving knowledge of our Lord. We are told in Ephesians 6:10-12 to "be strong in the Lord and in the strength of His might. Put on the full armor of God, that you may be able to stand firm against the schemes of the devil. For our struggle is not against flesh and blood, but against the rulers, against the powers, against the world forces of this darkness, against the spiritual forces of wickedness in the heavenly places."

We need to not only pray for our children's spiritual protection, but we also need to teach our children the principles of putting on God's armor. Just as we help them to dress physically, we should help them learn to dress spiritually as well.

To do this we need to teach them how to buckle the absolute truth of God's Word around themselves and to help them to memorize Scripture. For the breastplate of righteousness, we need to tell them the importance of protecting our hearts so that our motives and actions are pure. Their little feet need to be ready to go and share the good news of the gospel. The shield of faith will help them to defend the truth of God in a world that shoots flaming arrows of humanism and tolerance at all costs. The helmet of salvation helps to protect their minds so they can be single-minded for Christ and focus on Him always. Finally, the sword of the Spirit is to take those Scriptures written on the tablets of their hearts and help them to be bold enough to quote them and apply them in their daily lives. Just as we would never dream of sending our children out into the world without their physical clothing, we should never want them to leave God's armor behind either.

Other pirates are more subtle but no less destructive. They seem to dock in our ports and steal away the treasures of childhood so subtly we hardly know the hooligans are there. I've discovered them in my home at times, stealing our treasures. These renegades are called Distraction, Impatience, and Busyness.

Distraction

Distraction steals away precious times and opportunities to create memories and teach lessons. Have you ever set out to play ball with little Johnny only to feel the tug of the dishes in the sink? Has your elementary-aged child ever begged you to read a book with her with too many long words and too many pages? You start with good intentions, and then the telephone whisks you away. Or maybe your teenager begs you to let him practice driving, but it's quicker and a lot less stressful for you to drive.

"Maybe next time, dear." "When I have more time," you promise.

Oh, how I'm talking to myself! If ADHD had adult poster children, I would definitely be a candidate!

I've learned I have to get intentional with my time with the kids. I have to purposefully set aside time to be with them…really be with them. To combat the distractions that inevitably try to steal away my time, I have to enlist my children to help with housework. I also try to cook dinner earlier during the day so I don't have to juggle helping with homework and cooking at the same time. I also schedule individual date nights with each of my children so they have a designated block of time where they can count on my undivided attention.

Impatience

When I have too little time to accomplish too many to-dos, my fuse is way too short. I'm a pretty patient person until I get pushed a little too far and stretched a little too thin. Combine that with too little sleep, and impatience creeps in to wreak havoc on my home.

To combat impatience, I've learned I must get enough sleep. If that means taking a nap during the day or going to bed earlier, then so be it. I've also learned that I must say no to some things. Before I add anything to my schedule, I look to see how many other commitments I've made and decide whether to add this new item based on what's realistic. I've also learned to quit trying to do all things perfectly. While I like things done just so, it's not worth the stress to my family and me. Nothing is worth losing your patience over.

But if you feel you must scream, go outside and holler your head off to the trees. They will still be standing strong after you finish. Your children may not fare as well.

Busyness

Why is it so many moms feel compelled to involve their children in every activity imaginable? I saw a cartoon once that featured two kids trying to come up with a play date. Between piano lessons, soccer practice, choir rehearsal, ballet, and art classes, they could hardly find time to play. Involving kids in too many activities will steal away valuable time for children to just be children and for families to be families.

I saw my kids and me falling into Busyness's trap so I determined to slow down the pace of our lives. After much prayer, we felt led by God to homeschool several of our children which helped slow us all down. We need time to eat together and play together as a family. I want my kids to have time to let their imaginations develop during spontaneous play. I want us to have family devotions and devote time to developing our children's impressionable characters. While outside activities are good, they must be limited.

All mothers struggle at times to know how best to tuck treasures into their children's lives. But one thing I'm quick to do is ask God to show me the way I should go and what I should do. I'm careful to watch for pirates of all types and quick to scurry my little treasure hunters to safety when danger looms. I take this mothering thing one day at a time and do the best I can today.

Arrows in the Sand

When my kids were on the beach hunting for treasure, they were thankful for the arrows in the sand that pointed them in the right direction. The same is true on our parental treasure hunt. We need to set consistent guidelines and boundaries to keep us heading our children in the right direction. Before my husband and I set limits, life was a little crazy.

Take for instance the day I felt I might lose it at any minute. You know the kind of day I'm talking about. The baby is screaming, the older two are fighting, and I'm under the kitchen sink trying to figure out why a tidal wave has turned my kitchen into a swimming pool. No one is obeying me, and the whining—oh, the whining!

Tears well up in my eyes, my throat tightens, and I wonder where I might go to sign up for the next Thelma and Louise trip off the side of a cliff. I thought this motherhood thing was supposed to be fun and fulfilling. Where have I gone wrong? What's wrong with my children? What's wrong with me?

I want to be kind and gentle; so why do I sometimes scream at my children? I want to be nurturing; so why do I sometimes want to escape? I love my children; so why do I sometimes feel as though I don't like them very much?

After hearing about one too many days like this, my husband decided we needed to change the way we were tending our little sheep, and I agreed. So we decided to check out other flocks. We watched other shepherds and consulted many shepherding manuals. Most important, we sought out the Master Shepherd and gleaned from His eternal truths as we developed a plan for our pasture. The key word in that last sentence is "plan." We realized this fly-by-the-seat-of-our-pants parenting wasn't working, and it was time to get intentional with our shepherding.

So began our great sheep reformation. We put up fences and made the sheep aware of the consequences of stepping out of bounds. Instead of running wildly around the pasture, our sheep played within our established boundaries. As shepherds, we were loving and consistent, and soon everyone was enjoying greener pastures.

We have two simple rules for our household, two arrows in the sand that point the way our family plans to go. Our children can recite these by heart and will be quick to tell you what the consequences are for jumping a fence, so to speak.

Words and Actions

Rule # 1: Our words are kind and true, and our actions reflect what Jesus would do. Psalm 19:14 says, "Let the words of my mouth and the meditation of my heart be acceptable in Thy sight, O LORD, my rock and my redeemer."

I once heard James Dobson talk about sibling rivalry and how he and Shirley wouldn't allow hurtful things to be done and said in their home. He went on to explain that the home should be a safe haven where no one is threatened or hurt. He stood his two children in front of a window and pointed to the world outside. He told them that out in the world there would be people who would hurt them, but he wouldn't allow it within the walls of their home.

We in the TerKeurst family have adopted that policy and hold to it steadfastly. We often ask the children when conflict arises among them the popular catch phrase, "What would Jesus do?" His words and actions were kind, and we want that to be the pattern by which our children learn to treat others. We ask our children to try to resolve their conflicts among themselves first. If that isn't possible, they may seek our help, but not by tattling on one another. The offended sibling comes to one of us and simply states that the other needs to share what she has done. Then the offender tells us what has happened. Since the children know the consequences for wrong behaviors, we carry out the punishment they expect.

We also make a big deal about telling the absolute truth in our home. Any deceitfulness, either through blatant lies or through omissions, isn't tolerated. Our children know it's better to tell the truth, and we make it safe for them to do so. We've built trust with our children so they know what will happen when they are disobedient and that there will be no unfair surprises. This has helped them admit their wrong-doings rather than cover them up.

Listen and Obey

Rule # 2: We listen and obey quickly, quietly, with sweet, gentle spirits. When the children are asked to do something or to refrain from doing something, they know we expect their responses to be governed by this second rule. If any part of the rule is broken, there are consequences. The Bible states children are to obey their parents. Teaching them to listen and obey their earthly parents will create a path leading to obeying their heavenly Father.

Now, before your mind wanders off to the politically correct philosophy of tolerance, let me encourage you to expect obedience from your children. Building safe boundaries in your home will give your children more than just a knowledge of right and wrong. It will teach your child that Mommy and Daddy care enough to expect the very best behavior. It builds a child's self-esteem to feel loved and cared for. It gives freedom to know what the limits are. It gives confidence to have a clear understanding of what's expected of them and what the consequences are for disobedience.

Consequences are different for various offenses but always are governed by three simple principles: swift, severe, and covered in love. The swift part means the consequence is carried out immediately. The severe part means that the consequence will be remembered. Before visions of abuse start to flood your mind, please hold on because the third component governs the first two. Without exception, the punishment is covered in love. We don't discipline out of anger. We're controlled and calm as we carry out any consequence. Then afterwards we spend some quiet time with that child, holding them and reassuring them of our love.

Dr. Burton White, in a Harvard study, found the most effective parents were those who were firm disciplinarians while simultaneously showing love and affection for their children.[1] We've found that to be true, and while our children aren't perfect, they are obedient and well loved.

I'm not a child psychologist, but I've seen great results from this type of parenting. My desire is to raise my children in a way that honors and glorifies God.

But I'm in the middle of this child-rearing journey and have a long way to go before I rest. Sharon, on the other hand, is near the end of her parenting journey and has some wonderful insights to share from her perspective. After all, she wrote the book on motherhood…literally—*Being a Great Mom, Raising Great Kids*. So if you're the mother of teens and are past a lot of what I've just shared or are just eager to walk a little further into this adventure we call motherhood, sit back and enjoy some words from one I know is wise!

FIFTEEN

As Fences Fade

Sharon

I used to walk around the neighborhood and see signs that read, "Dog contained by invisible fence." I thought it was a joke. But after we added a dog to our family, I learned about this incredible invention and decided to have one installed.

The fence company dug a narrow, four-foot deep trench around the perimeter of our yard and buried a small wire. This wire was attached to a control box mounted on our garage wall. Ginger was then fitted with a collar sporting a special little box with two small prongs that rested against her skin. The dog trainer placed white flags all around the yard, marking where the underground fence was buried. As Ginger neared the flags, she heard a warning sound clicking from the box. When she kept going and crossed over the boundary marked by the flag, she received a shock and retreated.

Before you get upset about Ginger receiving a little shock, I have to tell you, I let them shock me first. It wasn't painful, but I didn't want them to do it again. In more than ten years Ginger has crossed over the boundary only twice—once when the fence wasn't working properly and once during her sixth week of motherhood to escape her seven nursing puppies. (Can't you relate!)

If you ride by our house today, you don't see any white flags decorating the perimeter of our yard. So, you might ask, how does Ginger know where the boundary is? For the first week, white flags lined the boundary of our yard. The second week, I removed every other flag. The third week, I removed every other remaining flag. The fourth week, I removed every other remaining flag. I continued removing flags until eventually all the flags were gone. We don't see the flags, but Ginger remembers where the boundaries are. She also learned that the warning sound was her friend and kept her from getting in a "shocking" situation.

Pulling Up the Flags

Lysa is in a stage of life with her children in which her home is lined with "flags" marking the boundaries. As children mature into adolescence, we pull up those flags, just a few at a time. As they graduate from high school and move into college, most of the flags marking the boundaries are gone, and we pray with all our might that our children remember where the boundaries are.

Just as Ginger hears the warning sound when she moves too close to danger, I believe the Holy Spirit taps on our children's hearts, warning them not to cross the boundaries set by their parents. Sometimes they will proceed and cross the boundary anyway. That's when the shock comes. It might be in the form of discipline, or it might be in the form of living with unpleasant consequences.

A young child is disciplined with a spanking or time out. An older child is disciplined by the removal of privileges, such as video games, phone, computer, weekend excursions with friends, car keys, and so on.

In the Old Testament, God wrote the law on tablets of stone, but in the New Testament He writes the law of love on our hearts. Isn't that our prayer as parents? Yes, we have to spell out the boundaries for our children and point them in the right direction. But as they head off to adulthood, we desire that the boundaries will be written on their hearts and they won't find themselves in shocking situations.

SIXTEEN

Buried Treasure: Taking the Time and Effort

LYSA

*S*ociety is used to thinking of treasure as jewels to be purchased, but your child's heart is a treasure that can't be bought. To touch that heart requires time plus effort and equals a nurtured child. God started to teach me this life lesson on motherhood one morning in a surprising way.

Family snuggle time is a tradition in the TerKeurst home. Many mornings our younger children sleepily make their way downstairs to crawl in bed with Mommy and Daddy to start their day with some good, old-fashioned snuggling. There are plenty of good morning kisses and giggles to go around.

On one such morning several years ago, Hope decided to play the piggy game with her little sister's toes. We've played this game many times, but her rhyme caught me by surprise. "This little piggy goes to aerobics, and this little piggy goes to a meeting. This little piggy goes to the grocery store, and this little piggy goes to swim lessons." I was tickled by her rendition of the familiar rhyme; however, I was struck that none of her piggies stayed home.[1]

Time

I decided we needed to rethink how we were spending our most precious commodity—time. Time to nurture and teach our children in the ways of the Lord. Time to sit and read. Time to play hide-and-go-seek, beauty shop, and cowboys and Indians. Time to share secrets. Time to kiss scraped knees and tear-stained faces. Time for imagination and childhood dreams. Time for listening about first loves and for comforting broken hearts. Time to cheer our children on to victory in all of life's races.

Don't get me wrong; I'm not saying going to aerobics, the grocery store, and meetings are bad things, except when they crowd out time with our children. Ecclesiastes 3:1 says, "There is an appointed time for everything. And there is a time for every event under heaven." Don't miss out on the precious time you have with your children today, because they are only young for a season.

I want Hope's piggy version to go something like this: "This little piggy played hide-and-go-seek and this one read stories. This one ran errands, and this one fixed dinner. But this one exclaimed, 'Yeah!' as we all headed home."

That's my purpose as a mother—to make home a place my children look forward to coming back to, a place where they know they are safe, loved, and accepted. I must be available and tuned in to whatever they are facing in their lives for that to be true.

All of this takes time and effort. You see, you can spend a lot of time just being around your kids taking care of them physically. But without a concerted effort to invest yourself in them emotionally, mentally, and spiritually, you will miss the mark of shaping the whole child. On the other hand, if you plan with great effort to develop your child in every way and involve him or her in loads of activities that keep your family out of the house every night of the week, you're missing out on the precious time it takes to really invest yourself in your child. The key is to balance your time together with the right efforts and cover everything in prayer.

U.S. News & World Report published an article called "Attention Must Be Paid" that revealed, "According to recent findings, the neuron links that are the keys to creativity and intelligence in later life are mainly laid down by the age of three. Is inherited ability the main factor in establishing this connection? Apparently not. Interactions with an attentive adult—in most cases, a mother—matter most."[2]

Effort

The Bible also teaches the importance of combining time with the right efforts in Deuteronomy 6:6-8. "These commandments that I give you today are to be upon your hearts. Impress them on your children. Talk about them when you sit at home and when you walk along the road, when you lie down and when you get up" (NIV). We must take the time the Bible is talking about and combine it with the effort it takes to teach our children God's Word.

Notice the first part of verse 6 instructs parents to place God's Word on their hearts. Only when we have a personal and ongoing relationship with the perfect parent, our heavenly Father, can we be properly prepared to train up our children.

Notice the word "impress" in verse 7. To impress God's Word on our children is more than just telling them about God. It's modeling God's Word in our lives and making our relationship with Him apparent to our children. They need to see us reading His Word. They need to hear us pray. They need to see us being kind to others and acting out His precepts in our everyday lives. Only when they see us living out what we are teaching them about God will we impress God's commands on their hearts, where the true treasure is buried.

Sometimes we think teachable moments only come during carefully planned family worship times. But I think that, while those times are important, it is as our children see us living out our relationship with God in the middle of everyday life that lasting impressions can be made.

For example, one day I needed to pick up Hope from school, but my car wouldn't start. I tried five or six times to pump the accelerator. I even begged it to please start. Then I decided to go back into the house and call my husband to see if he could pick up Hope. He was out of the office on an appointment. Tearfully I sat in the driver's seat and prayed aloud for God to please let my car start and help us to make it to Hope's school. Afterward I glanced in the backseat only to find my other two daughters, Ashley and Brooke, intently watching me.

Please, God, let them see You answer this prayer, I thought, as I turned the key. The car started as if nothing had ever been wrong.

Ashley exclaimed, "Yeah, God answered our prayer!" I closed my eyes and thanked God for that moment.

Many days I'm not sure I'm doing a good job of being a parent. But that day God showed me that, while I'm not perfect, if I consistently turn to the One who is, I can make godly impressions on my children.

With time and effort, my small parenting offerings are taken by God and used to reach the treasure of my children's hearts, to teach my children He is a loving and caring Father who will always be there for them. For that I am deeply grateful.

SEVENTEEN

The Map

SHARON

*B*efore our son was born, Steve and I took a parenting class at the Red Cross. I learned how to change a diaper without puncturing the doll's leg with a diaper pin, how to hold a bottle so the wee one wouldn't get air bubbles in his tummy, and how to retrieve nondigestibles that babies feel compelled to put into their mouths. But you can't learn some things in a class.

On February 4, 1984, Steven Hugh Jaynes Junior came screaming into the world. Oh, he didn't want to come but hung on to my insides for all he was worth. But after twenty-three hours, the inevitable occurred, and he was forced to make his debut.

I interpreted his cries for all those in earshot. He was saying, "I don't like it out here! Who let the water out of my pool? Where's the guy who squeezed my head? Let me at him! Shiver me timbers, somebody get me a blanket! It's cold out here! Get that light out of my eyes, for goodness' sakes! Stop poking at me already!"

Then the nurse placed the little bundle on my chest, and he immediately quieted. We locked eyes, and he seemed to say, "Hey, I know you. You're my mommy."

When I looked at the seven pounds, eight ounces of love that lay in my arms drawing nourishment from my body, I realized that nourishing him body, soul, and spirit was an honor and a privilege bestowed on me by my heavenly Father. In the following days, months, and years, some aspects of mothering came naturally, others did not. I read many books, watched other mothers, and talked endlessly with the only perfect parent I could find—God.

A Blessed Mother

Proverbs 31:28 says that the wife of noble character has children that "arise and call her blessed" (NIV).

"Oh, God," I prayed, "show me how to be a mother like that." I didn't want to be honored at a banquet, with my child standing before a crowd giving me accolades. But I desired to do my best, to give mothering my all, and to raise a child who loved the Lord with all his heart.

Through the years, I've noted seven qualities of good mothering that come up time and time again, and I've outlined them in my book *Being a Great Mom, Raising Great Kids.* While I can't include that book in this book, I can give you a sampling and show you how to find out more from the map that is laid out in God's Word.

Be a Beacon

A mother whose children arise and call her blessed is much like a stately lighthouse. She has a solid foundation in Jesus Christ. Her walls of faith are constructed to withstand the storms of life, and her primary function is to house the light of Christ. This mother is an immovable constant in her child's life, a landmark along life's journey, and a guiding light that points her children to the safe harbor of home and eventually out to sea.[1]

I often hear people say, "Women wear many hats today." But quite honestly, I don't own a hat, and I think it's easier to talk about our roles through the types of shoes we wear: bedroom slippers, tennis shoes, sandals, clogs, boots, flats, pumps, and heels. We own a variety of colors and styles to suit every mood, occasion, and outfit. My side of the closet is packed with shoes representing my various roles. However, my husband's side of the closet has four pairs in a neat little row: brown loafers, black loafers, running shoes, and golf shoes. My husband works hard, but his roles are more defined and succinct than mine.

We moms have hectic schedules. Sometimes my life consists of flitting back and forth from one thing to the other so quickly I feel like a switchboard operator in an old black-and-white movie. "Peanut butter and jelly? Just one moment please. Cough syrup? Just one moment please. Money for the concert? Just one moment please. A ride to practice? Just one moment please. PTA? Just one moment please. No one's answering. Would you like to leave a message?"

Even though moms in this new millennium are on the go as never before, we can still assure our children that our love never changes, our support never tires, and our commitment to being a beacon remains unmoved. A beacon mom is a guiding light to her children that is present, available, and approachable. And she's an unmovable landmark on life's journey. If a child becomes lost, he knows he can search for the landmark to show him the way home.

The beacon is a landmark that her children can always count on. She is watching out over the sea of faces to protect her tiny fleet. The Proverbs 31 woman "watches over the affairs of her household" (verse 27a NIV). She is present. She's available. And she's on guard.

The words "watches over" mean "to hedge about as with thorns," much like a mother bird might do to protect her young. These same words are also used in the Bible as a military term, such as to watch over a city.[2] Can't you see it now, the lighthouse standing tall, not rocked by the surf, guiding her children safely to shore?

But this beacon watches out for more than the physical safety of her fleet. She watches out for their spiritual and emotional needs as well. Her gaze is not a casual glance.

She doesn't just give her children a "once over" before they rush out the door to make sure their hair is combed and their socks match. This is a mother who guards, protects, saves, guides, and attends to those precious to her.[3]

Climbing to the top of a lighthouse can be a dizzying, laborious task, just as raising one's children can be. But keep in mind, the real view is at the top.

Be a Listener

Research shows mothers who work outside the home spend fewer than eleven minutes a day conversing with their kids, and stay-at-home moms spend about thirty minutes.[4] Now, assuming that half of that time the parent is doing the talking, that brings the listening time to five-and-a-half and fifteen minutes. I've always been taught that as long as I'm talking, I'm not learning. If we want our children to call us blessed, we are going to have to learn how to listen to what they have to say.

A mother whose children arise and call her blessed listens with her whole being. She listens with her eyes, putting down the dust cloth and looking into the eyes of her child. She listens with her ears, tuning in with her radar and all the homing devices God has provided. She listens with her facial expressions, communicating that no request is too silly and no question too insignificant. She listens with her lips, entering in the conversation without judging but showing genuine interest in what is being said. She listens with her mind, asking great questions that draw the child out and creates an atmosphere of sharing and trust. And she listens with her heart, tuning in to unspoken hurts, pressures, and desires.

Recently, I was with a group of mothers of teenagers who were bemoaning how their teens weren't talking to them as much as they had in the past. I think we're unrealistic to expect teenagers to spill out their hearts and tell their parents all of their problems.

120

My son and I had a precious relationship before he hit adolescence. Then, suddenly, just a few months after he entered middle school, I noticed a change. He was talking less and pulling away.

Proverbs 20:5 says "the purposes of a man's heart are deep waters, but a man [mom] of understanding draws them out" (NIV). We can draw out our children by using our minds and our mouths to ask good questions. These aren't interrogation questions to gather information but questions that show genuine interest and support.

Robert Crosby said, "Ambassadors use questions to build bridges between countries that are oceans apart. Teachers use questions to build bridges to their students. Spouses use questions to build intimacy with one another. Managers use questions to cultivate teamwork and productivity among employees."[5] Wise parents use questions to bridge the generation divide with their children, whether en route to nursery school or on the way home from a high school soccer game.

Here are a few questions to get you started.

- What is the hardest part about being (fill in your child's age)?

- What do you think heaven looks like?

- What does Dad do at work?

- Who is a person you know who seems the most Christlike?

- What do you think your wife (husband) will be like?

- If you were going to spend one year on a desert island and could only take three things with you, what would they be?

- If people followed the Golden Rule, think of all the things we wouldn't need. Can you make a list?

- If you could be in a movie that you've already seen, which one would it be? Would you be a character who's already in the movie, or would you be one you would add?

- How is love different for a Christian couple than it is in the movies?

- What's the difference between being smart and being wise?

- When you pray, how do you picture God?

Be an Encourager

On the way to one of Steven's cross-country races, I got lost. (This is no surprise to my friends.) The races only last about twenty minutes so it's important to be on time. Well, I arrived just as the runners were walking off the trail.

On the way home, Steven said, "You know, so many parents and fans were cheering for the other teams, but hardly anybody yelled for us. When I ran by and heard them cheering for everyone else, it actually made me go slower. I didn't think it would really matter that much, but it did."

A mother is a cheerleader whose voice can pump courage and confidence into her children's heart. She's the cheerleader on the sidelines who knows that an uplifting word, offered at the right moment, could make the difference between her children finishing well or collapsing along the way.[6]

Imagine this scenario: Your child gets up in the morning and dresses in a shingled outfit of paper, much like Post-It notes. Every time you question your daughter's worth, criticize her, make her feel guilty, incapable, insufficient, or unattractive, a piece of paper drops to the ground. When you see the slip of paper flutter to the floor, perhaps you realize the effect of your words and try to stick the paper back on with a positive word. However, it won't stick. The child goes off to school and hears more discouraging words. Finally, at the end of the day, she comes home, exposed and insecure— and rightly so.

Her soul stands naked.

Studies show that, in the average home, ten negative comments are made for every positive one. Also, it takes four positive comments to counteract one negative statement. With that ratio, it's easy to understand why so many children are discouraged and have poor self-images.[7]

A mother cheers for her child beginning at the moment she holds her infant in her arms. She speaks sweetly to her new charge. With her eyes locked on her child's, she silently speaks volumes about the treasure she has cradled to her breast. The blessed mother is the mirror that reflects love back to the child and says, "You are special and valuable to me."

The blessed mother cheers for the bundle of joy when the baby rolls over, laughs, and kicks her tiny feet into the air. The mom even gives a hurrah when the baby burps! (My, how things change from infancy to puberty!) She encourages the baby when he shakes a rattle, holds a cup, points to a color, and responds to his name. But mostly she praises the child for no reason at all except "just because you're mine."

If we leave our child's cheering section, if our seat is vacant, the child will look for someone else to fill it. That someone is usually a peer. Then the child tries to please whoever is occupying that seat in the stands. So dust off those pom-poms! Ready that megaphone! Be about the business of becoming your child's greatest fan![8]

Be a Self-Esteem Builder

One of my favorite cartoon strips is *Peanuts*. In one strip, Charlie Brown is standing at Lucy's psychiatric booth getting a little helpful advice. Lucy says, "Don't build your house on the sand, Charlie Brown." Then a gust of wind comes and blows Lucy, Charlie, and her booth up into the air, to land in a crumpled heap. In the final frame she concludes, "Or use cheap nails."

A mother whose children arise to call her blessed is a self-esteem builder. She builds on the solid rock of Jesus Christ with a foundation of unconditional love and acceptance. She constructs a framework, making the child feel capable, valuable, and with a strong sense of belonging. She adds the insulation of affection and locks and bolts to keep out the enemy. She doesn't use the cheap nails of the world such as beauty and performance but constructs a sturdy house built on our value in Jesus Christ.

Giving encouragement and building self-esteem are kissing cousins. Encouragement builds someone up and gives him courage. Building self-esteem helps a child to be strong and to see himself in a proper perspective.

Self-esteem is how a person feels about himself, how much he likes who he is, how comfortable he is with his weaknesses, and how in tune he is to his strengths. And it's biblical.

Understanding who you are in Christ gives great confidence. This understanding also keeps us from pride, as we realize we haven't done anything to attain such a heavenly inheritance. Jesus did it for us. We have great worth, not because of who we are, but because of whose we are, and that keeps self-esteem in proper perspective.

Self-esteem isn't conceit. Someone with proper self-esteem is so comfortable with who he is and the value he has as a child created in God's image that he has no need to impress others. But self-esteem based on appearance and performance causes pride.

Young David in the Bible is a wonderful example of a person who found his value in being a child of God. In 1 Samuel 17, David, who was probably a young teenager at the time, went to the battlefield where the Israelite army was in a standoff with the Philistines. David had arrived with provisions for his brothers, who were in the Israelite army. But he saw how afraid the soldiers were of Goliath, a giant on the opposing side.

He asked the men, "Who is this uncircumcised Philistine, that he should taunt the armies of the living God?" (verse 26b). In other words, who does Goliath think he is? David wasn't conceited or trying to impress anyone, but he knew God could work through him. So he fought the giant when no one else was willing. David said, "The LORD who delivered me from the paw of the lion and from the paw of the bear, He will deliver me from the hand of this Philistine" (verse 37). And God did.

Be a Seed Sower

My grandfather was a farmer, and several of his children followed in his muddy footsteps. One thing I learned from watching my aunts and uncles as a little girl is that a farmer never plants the seeds and then leaves them alone, hoping for the best. No, he "tends" the land. With all the modern farm equipment today, such as combines, backhoes, and harvesters, the word "tend" has lost its significance. But this precious word exemplifies a mother's "tend-er" care.

The mother whose children arise and call her blessed is a seed sower. She gathers good seeds from God's Word and presses them into the fertile soil of her children's hearts. She fertilizes the seeds with encouraging words, spurring her charges to grow to their fullest potential. And she waters the seeds daily with prayer. Then one day, the tender shoots burst forth, resulting in a bounty of fruit, and the seed sower celebrates the rewards of her labor.[9]

Sowing seeds of Scripture and prayer can be just as natural as breathing. It can consist of praising God for a beautiful sunset, thanking Him for our food, or praying for a skinned knee.

You can start the planting as soon as a child is born. When you rock the babe in your arms, tell her how much Jesus loves her. When you bathe him in the sink, tell about how Jesus washes away our sins. When you comb her hair, tell about how God knows every hair on her head. When a test is coming up, pray with your student to do his best.[10]

We have a very short window of time to tend the tender fields of our child's heart. Just as there is a time to plant and a time to reap, we must not miss the planting season, or the harvest will be sparse. As Hannah Whitehall Smith once said, "For the mother is and must be, whether she knows it or not, the greatest, strongest, and most lasting teacher her children ever have."[11]

Be an Example Setter

I was amazed when my son obtained his driver's permit and I saw how he slung the car around a corner, cutting it close as he turned into our neighborhood—just as he had seen me do for fifteen years. Regardless of what we say to our children, or what values we attempt to instill in their hearts, nothing speaks louder than our actions. We can plant the seeds with our words, but they won't take root unless our walk matches our talk. A mother whose children arise and call her blessed is an example setter who demonstrates love, joy, peace, patience, kindness, goodness, faithfulness, gentleness, and self-control in her own life.[12]

You might notice these character traits as the fruit of the Spirit, found in Galatians 5:22-23. If we demonstrate these traits in our lives, then the phrase "the fruit doesn't fall far from the tree" will be a blessing and not a curse.

Recently I read a portion of *It's Always Something,* by the late Gilda Radner, which exemplifies how important a mother's example can be.

When I was little, my nurse Dibby's cousin had a dog, just a mutt, and the dog was pregnant. I don't know how long dogs are pregnant, but she was due to have her puppies in about a week. She was out in the yard one day and got in the way of the lawn mower and her two hind legs got cut off. They rushed her to the vet and he said, "I can sew her up, or you can put her to sleep if you want, but the puppies are okay. She'll be able to deliver the puppies."

Dibby's cousin said, "Keep her alive."

So the vet sewed up her backside, and over the next week the dog learned to walk. She didn't spend any time worrying; she just learned to walk by taking two steps in the front and flipping up her backside, and then taking two steps and flipping up her backside again. She gave birth to six little puppies, all in perfect health. She nursed them and then weaned them. And when they learned to walk, they all walked like her.[13]

Our children are watching, and chances are, they will walk just like us.

Be Diligent

I was at a speaking engagement when someone handed me a poem, written by a diligent mother.

> *I'll stand in the gap for my son.*
> *I'll stand till the victory's won.*
> *This one thing I know*
> *That You love him so,*
> *And Your work with my child is not done.*
>
> *I'll stand in the gap every day,*
> *And there I will fervently pray;*

And, Lord, just one favor
Don't let me waver
If things get quite rough, which they may.

I'll never give up on that boy.
Nor will You, for You promised him joy.
For I know it was true
When he said "Yes" to You,
Though the enemy seeks to destroy.

I'll not quit as I intercede,
For You are His Savior, indeed!
Though it may take years,
I give You my fears,
As I trust every moment I plead.

And so in the gap I will stand,
Heeding Your every command,
With help from above,
I'll unconditionally love,
And soon he will reach for Your hand.
—Shirley Pope Waite

The seventh key ingredient of a mother whose children arise and call her blessed is that she is diligent. She doesn't give up but keeps pressing on toward the goal of raising godly children; she doesn't give in but sticks to a strategic plan of discipline; and she understands that ultimately life decisions must be made by the child, so she gives her child over to God.

The map for discovering the treasure buried in every child's heart is God's Word. As mothers, we have access to the map, and in turn become the map for our child. As we follow His example, not only do we guide our children to discovering rare and wonderful treasures, but we also become known as a treasure. As Proverbs 31:10 says, "An excellent wife, who can find? For her worth is far above jewels."

EIGHTEEN

A Contented Mother

SHARON

A few years ago I fell in love with a beach cottage named "Barb's Folly." I adored the designer beach décor of stripes and floral prints; the screened-in porch that spanned the back of the house; the inviting, dark green rocking chairs, and the weatherworn dock jutting out over the lazy canal.

As if imported from England, a six-foot square of grass was nestled in one corner of the white picket fence in the back, with blooming myrtle bushes, a weathered bench, and a cozy birdhouse. In the other corner of the yard, the owners had planted a palm tree, just a few inches from the second-story wraparound porch.

On our first night there, we sat on the porch and rocked in the chairs, watching the fireflies dance under the moonlight on the canal. At one point, a moonbeam fell across the palm tree, and I noticed something stir. When I moved closer, I discovered a turtledove had built her nest at the top of the thatched tree trunk, where the palm branches spouted upward. Because we were on the second story, we were at eye level with Mrs. Turtle Dove.

When I moved closer to her, she didn't budge but sat steadfast in her perch. Early the next morning, I went onto the porch to spend some time with the Lord, and Mrs. Turtle Dove was there to greet me. I rocked. She watched.

Our eyes locked. We both blinked. Then, around 8:30, Mr. Turtle Dove flew in and perched on the stairwell railing. They exchanged coos, and after a few moments, he flew over to the nest. When she stood up to welcome him, I noticed two tiny eggs peeking out from under the stubble.

It seems this was mother's morning out. She flew away, and Daddy bird took over the incubation of the offspring for his lady love. After a brief time, she returned, and Daddy bird went off to work for the rest of the day.

During our vacation, the momma dove did one thing and one thing only—she rested in the palm, warming and protecting her two tiny charges. On the afternoon when a violent storm blew through with loud claps of thunder, crackling flashes of lightning, and pelting sheets of rain, she just sat there, resting in the palm, undaunted by the storm.

When children ran up and down the stairs, inches from her nest, she just sat there, unalarmed by the activity. While other birds such as cranes, pelicans, and seagulls performed great feats, swooping gracefully into the water to retrieve their catch of the day, she just sat there, undeterred from her calling.

On the last morning of our vacation, I was having a final cup of coffee on the back porch. It was just God, Mrs. Turtle Dove, and me.

Because I believe God puts various situations in front of us for a reason, I asked, "God, what do you want me to learn from watching this mother bird this week?"

Then He spoke to my heart. It was contentment. I was watching a picture of contentment in fulfilling God's call. The contentment of a mother doing what God had fashioned her to do. Regardless of the storms, regardless of what other seemingly more audacious birds were doing around her, regardless of the endless stream of activity passing by her nest, she was unmoved from her calling during this time in her life.

"Is that it, Lord? Is that what you're showing me?" Just as I prayed those words, Mr. Turtle Dove came in for his daily visit. When his lady dove stood up to fly away, I noticed a piece of eggshell attached to her leg. I peeked in the nest, and there lay two downy hatchlings. It was as if God were saying to me, "Yes, Sharon, that's it. This has been My gift to you this week. You've seen a contented mother and the results of her commitment. You do what I've called you to do. Rest in the palm of My hand. Don't get distracted by the world and all the activity that's going on around you. Be undaunted by the storms. Be relentless in your call. And in due time I will cause your 'eggs to hatch,' and all too soon they will leave the nest."

About that time, my six-foot-one teenage son sleepily stumbled out onto the porch. I'm not sure if he saw the tears in my eyes as I looked at his ruffled hair, sleepy eyes, and a face that needed a shave.

"Hey, Bud, look. The eggs hatched today."

Splashes from John

SHARON

*T*he Proverbs 31 woman believes that motherhood is a high calling with the responsibility of shaping and molding the children who will one day define who we are as a community and a nation. That, my friends, can be a little overwhelming at times. But I have good news for you: While we can be great parents, we will never be perfect parents. We won't always be available beacons. At times we won't pay attention or listen as we should. We will sometimes offer discouraging words and occasionally be part of the wrecking crew instead of building self-esteem. Some days we'll inadvertently sow weeds instead of planting seeds, occasionally set a bad example, and at times we'll become lackadaisical and put diligence on the shelf.

I know these aren't inspiring words, but they are reality. How do I know this? Because I am a member of the IPC, the Imperfect Parent Club.

There is only one perfect parent, and, in John 3, Jesus tells us how to become one of His children. Nicodemus was a Pharisee, a ruler, and a very religious man. He wanted to know more about Jesus so he crept away from his associates in the night for a private meeting. Nick admitted to

Jesus, "Rabbi, we know that You have come from God as a teacher; for no one can do these signs that You do unless God is with him" (verse 2).

Before Nick could even ask his first question, Jesus cut right to the chase. "Truly, truly, I say to you, unless one is born again, he cannot see the kingdom of God" (verse 3).

One might think Jesus' response had nothing to do with what Nicodemus was talking about. However, God knows the thoughts and intentions of our hearts. He knew what Nick was thinking, even if it didn't match what came out of his mouth. How like a parent!

Nicodemus's response to Jesus' statement shows his mind was exactly where Jesus had known it to be. "How can a man be born when he is old? He cannot enter a second time into his mother's womb and be born, can he?" (verse 4).

Jesus gave this explanation, "Truly, truly, I say to you, unless one is born of water and the Spirit, he cannot enter into the kingdom of God" (verse 5). Jesus leads us to the water once again. As babies, we swim around in the amniotic fluid of our mother's womb, pass through the birth canal, and become the child of our earthly parents. At rebirth, our spirits pass from darkness to light, and we become the children of our heavenly Father.

Physical birth, just like everything in the physical realm, can be seen, touched, and experienced with all the senses. Spiritual birth, like everything in the spiritual realm, must be believed and accepted by faith. However, in both the physical and spiritual realms, we're born as babes.

What a comfort to be the child of a perfect parent. He is a beacon who never leaves or forsakes us (Hebrews 13:5). He listens when we talk to Him (Psalm 34:4). He encourages us with love letters (Psalm 119:11). He causes seeds to bring forth a bountiful harvest in our lives (1 Corinthians 3:6).

His Son mirrors the Father as an ultimate example for us (Hebrews 1:3). And He is diligent in His love and intercession for us (Hebrews 7:25).

Yes, we are mothers. But we are also children. What a freeing thought.

Create a Loving Environment for Family and Friends

NINETEEN

Welcoming Jesus into Our Homes

SHARON

*P*rinciple 4: The Proverbs 31 woman is a disciplined and industrious keeper of the home who creates a warm and loving environment for her family and friends.

One of Jesus' favorite places to rest and refresh himself was in the little town of Bethany, nestled on the Mount of Olives, just two miles from Jerusalem. In particular, he enjoyed the home of Lazarus and his two sisters, Mary and Martha. They had the sort of place that spoke of welcome, warmth, and love.

What made their house so special? I doubt that designer drapes, fine china, or gourmet dinners put their abode on the home tour. I suspect instead a spirit of love and loveliness invited Christ in and beckoned Him to linger.

Mary and Martha had a Proverbs 31 kind of home, the sort that provided warmth and a loving environment to family and friends. I want a home like that, don't you? Let's look at what Mary and Martha did to create such a haven.

- Martha welcomed Jesus into her home (Luke 10:38), even going out to meet Him before He reached the house (John 11:20).

- Mary sat at Jesus' feet and listened intently to what He had to say (Luke 10:39).

- Martha prepared food for her guests and had a servant's heart (Luke 10:40). Please don't get hung up on Jesus' reprimand of Martha in Luke 10:41. I believe He was not discouraging her from serving but encouraging her not to let the function of serving overshadow the purpose of serving, leading others to Christ.

- Martha believed in Christ and His mighty power and wasn't afraid to share her beliefs (John 11:27).

- Mary brought others to meet Jesus and used her home as a place for evangelism (John 11:29-31).

Have you ever gone into a convenience store to pay for gas only to return smelling like cigarette smoke? Or have you ever hugged someone who had doused herself with a generous portion of perfume, and when you walked away, you were wearing the scent yourself? Mary and Martha had the type of home that was so filled with the fragrance of Christ, I imagine their guests left wearing His scent. I know on one particular occasion that was the case.

Jesus so loved this little home in Bethany that He spent His last week before the crucifixion there. Mary, moved by her great love for Him, poured costly perfume on His feet and wiped them with her hair. Her act of sacrificial love filled the room with a fragrance that, no doubt, permeated the very clothes of her guests and lingered for hours.

I want a home that so emanates the fragrance of Christ that everyone who leaves carries His scent with him. Don't you? Let's sit by the fourth pool and reflect on how we can make that dream home a reality. And while we're thinking, Lysa will show us how to invite in the presence of some very important guests to help to make that dream come true.

TWENTY

Making Your House a Home

LYSA

everal years ago some friends and I trekked over to an annual event in our city called Home-a-rama. I took a notepad and camera, hoping to walk away with a plethora of home-decorating ideas. But as we strolled through each of the beautifully and expensively decorated model homes, I grew ever more discouraged about my own home.

Even if I could afford such lavish decorations, my home would never look as picture perfect as these. No hair was on the bathroom tiles. No crayon marks and smudged handprints appeared on the walls. No cookie crumbs or puzzle pieces nestled underneath and in between the couch cushions. The fireplace had no ashes, the flowerbeds had no weeds, and no junk existed in the most logical place for a junk drawer in the kitchen.

Oh, to live in such a neat, organized, and beautiful home would be heaven on earth, I thought.

As we left the decorators' showcase, I noticed a small flyer on the table beside the exiting walkway. It promoted a big sale to be held the day after the completion of Home-a-rama. I marked the date on my calendar and could hardly wait to return for the sale.

Soon the big day arrived. By the time I got there, I was stunned to find that most of the houses didn't resemble the showcases they had been just days earlier. The designers had cleared out or sold many of the beautiful furnishings. I did find a lamp and a silk plant for a good price, so I bought them and left.

As I drove away from the houses I had coveted, I asked God to forgive me. I realized those houses were façades. All the details I had seen as blessings—no crumbs, smudges, or ashes—were signs that no life was being lived inside those houses. For they weren't homes at all. They were simply brick and mortar, wood and nails that had been fashioned with beautiful coverings, but the one item that makes a home truly wonderful, the heart, wasn't there.

Emilie Barnes, a leading Christian expert on home and time management, says, "Homes are not static monuments to taste. They're not museums. They are simply the stage where we experience the drama of our lives and where we invite others to share it with us."[1]

Our first logo at Proverbs 31 Ministries was a drawing of a house with a heart in the middle. The heart is essential because without it the home is simply a house. We believe that, just as the man is the home's head, the woman is the home's heart. Our motto is "Touching women's hearts, building godly homes." For we have seen over and over again that a woman sets the tone in her house, whether it be positive or negative. We desire to touch a woman's heart with Christ's love because we know what a wonderful effect that can have on her home life.

Turning a house into a home is more about the presence of a beautiful heart than wallpaper, paint, and neatly organized closets. While the world tells women, "If you have the right house, you'll be happy," I say, "If you have the right heart, your home will be happy no matter what kind of house you live in."

To be homekeepers who set a happy and rich tone in their houses, what kind of hearts should we have? Well, if we were having a party in our hearts and making out our guest list, five essential guests of honor would be invited. These would be love, peace, beauty, tradition, and hospitality. Having the presence of these guests would make your heart happy and your home a wonderful place to be. And the best part of all, this party would never end, for these guests can take up permanent residence and make your home the haven you and your family long for.

Now, let's explore what each of these guests brings to our homes to add warmth and heartfelt richness.

Proverbs 4:23 says, "Watch over your heart with all diligence, for from it flow the springs of life." As we explore the fourth pool in our cascade of seven, we find Scripture telling us that, when we keep a faithful watch over our homes, we must start by keeping a faithful watch over our hearts.

Inviting in Love

To invite love to our house party, it must be in our hearts so abundantly that it spills forth into our homes. Love is ultimately what makes a house a home. Love quiets the cry of the baby. Love kisses a toddler's scraped knee. Love plays dress up and Superman even though a zillion to-dos still reside on her list. Love stays up half the night to help her junior higher finish a school project. Love comforts a teen's broken heart. Love gives without expectation. Love sacrifices without hesitation. Love comes straight from heaven and lets us catch glimpses of our eternal home.

To fill your home with love is to invite in the very presence of God. A woman can never do and be all that is required of a wife, mother, and friend, without love filling and refilling her constantly. The only love I know of that can do that without ceasing is God's love. The Bible tells us that He will never leave us or forsake us, that His love is never ending, and that He loves us so much He sacrificed His only Son so we could know Him intimately and personally and have life everlasting. This awesome truth never ceases to amaze me.

I look at my children, and I know I would go to any extreme to protect them. I can't fathom allowing them to be sacrificed for even my best friend, much less for those who reject and hate me. Yet God loves us that much. That's the love that will sustain you, protect you, and give you wisdom in being a faithful keeper of your home.

That love is also an endangered species. As you comb through Scriptures you see that our society is becoming more and more characteristic of the last days. Second Timothy 3:1-4 says, "But mark this: There will be terrible times in the last days. People will be lovers of themselves, lovers of money, boastful, proud, abusive, disobedient to their parents, ungrateful, unholy, without love, unforgiving, slanderous, without self-control, brutal, not lovers of the good, treacherous, rash, conceited, lovers of pleasure rather than lovers of God" (NIV). Sound like you're reading the daily paper?

Notice that verse 3 says "without love." That phrase means "absent of family love" if you go back to the original Hebrew.[2] That's why it's more important than ever to fill our homes with the kind of love that can be a safe haven for our family and a refreshing oasis for others who may come to visit. In these latter times, a home filled with God's love is precious and rare but needed more than ever.

May we fill our hearts with God's love so that all who cross our thresholds feel His presence in our hearts and in our homes.

Inviting in Tradition

If making a home were like making a cake, love would be all that makes the cake sweet, and tradition would be the icing on top. To invite tradition into your home is to bring that little something extra that makes experiences memorable.

Think about a child's birthday cake. The colorful and tasty icing is what draws a child's eyes, excites the taste buds, and is often the highlight of the party. In the same way, establishing traditions will draw a family closer and keep each member enthusiastic about all that makes a family unique. Traditions are often the highlights recalled first in the vast catalog of family memories.

Everyone is born with a desire to belong. This need is especially evident in children. If a child finds the need met at home, he or she won't wander outside the safety of the family to find it. If, on the other hand, the child has no sense of belonging, he or she will look elsewhere.

This is where tradition comes in. Having special family traditions that model biblical principles will do more for a child's sense of belonging than anything else. It brings a sense of purpose to your family's activities and helps us to pause in the midst of busy times to keep celebrations special. A child knows he or she can count on celebrating life's victories and occasions with those closest to the heart. And tradition celebrates family. What confidence a kid feels, knowing home is a safe and wonderful place.

In my home we have several favorite traditions. We have a family night once a week that's reserved for our interaction. We might go to a special restaurant, stay at home and play games, go out in our pajamas for a late night ice cream run, or pop popcorn and watch an old movie. We weave discussions about important life issues into our time and talk about what God's Word says. A great resource for family night ideas is Focus on the Family's Heritage Builders, "Family Night Tool Box." We have some of the books in this series, and they are wonderful idea generators.

We also celebrate special events in each family member's life. We have a "You Are Special" red plate that the "guest of honor" is served dinner on and a red photo album in which the event is recorded with pictures and journaling.

One of my favorite simple traditions is our family's own hand signal that means "I love you" and special nicknames for each of our kids that express our sentiment in a playful and special way. Of course holidays are great times to practice family traditions, because these naturally lend themselves to family togetherness and memory making.

Whatever your traditions and whenever you carry them out, you're doing something much more important than event planning. You're letting your family members know they are important enough to establish special times that will tug on their heartstrings for years to come.

If the concept of family traditions is new to you, let me encourage you that, no matter what stage of life you are in, it's never too late to start. I've even known grandmothers who never had special traditions in their homes until the little pitter-patter of grandchildren came across their thresholds. I've also known people who had no children of their own but reached out to their nieces, nephews, and neighborhood children to make a positive impact and wonderful memories for those children. Whatever your circumstance or situation, whether the kids are two or twenty-two, you can make your home a wonderful place by inviting tradition in.

Inviting in Beauty

Most women love to bring beauty to their surroundings. I've heard it said that we are most like the Creator when we are creating. What better place to express our creativity and our unique personalities than in our homes? To take a shell of a house and fill it with splashes of color, touches of coziness, and inviting smells all harmonized with a sense of order will bring pleasure not only to the eye but also to the soul.

What could be more wonderful than to walk in your front door and feel welcomed home? Maybe it's the precious memories captured in picture frames throughout. Maybe it's being so familiar with every nook and cranny that you could make your way through your home blindfolded. Maybe it's the voices of your loved ones that have filled its halls so long you can almost still hear them echoing even when it's silent. There's just something special about that place we call home.

To invite beauty into this place will take time, if you're just starting out. God wouldn't be honored if you went into debt to beautify your home. With patience and creativity, you can do a lot with a little.

When we first settled into our home, the move wasn't complicated. We had two dressers, two beds without headboards or footboards, and some rent-to-own couches that originated in my husband's college apartment. We also had a washer but no dryer and a dog kennel. After we situated our sparse furniture, I became overwhelmed at the thought of transforming this place into the beautiful pictures floating around in my mind.

One day, as I was sharing my frustrations with a friend of mine, she suggested I take it slow and determine to save up money to purchase things with cash rather than credit. She suggested making a wish list of items I wanted for my home and asking my husband for these items for birthday and Christmas gifts. My husband and I also designated a certain amount of money each month for household purchases.

Before long I had enough money to buy one item. Where in the world would I start? I went to furniture stores and walked away overwhelmed at how much it would cost to furnish a whole room. Then I went to fabric stores and felt overwhelmed at all the choices. So I went to the bookstore and decided to read up on how the professionals did it.

I walked away from my research time with two great nuggets of decorating wisdom. The first was that I needed a palette of colors. I was to find one piece of colorful fabric that I felt drawn to. The colors in this fabric would become the colors I would decorate my home in. Paint choices, wallpaper choices, and fabrics for window treatments and upholstered furniture would need to all blend and coordinate with my palette.

Second, I discovered that some of the most beautifully decorated rooms weren't ones in which the furniture was purchased all at once but rather collected over the years.

So I went back to the fabric store, carefully chose a pattern that would serve as my palette, and bought one-fourth of a yard of it. I then purchased a three-ring notebook and started to collect pictures of the types of furniture and window treatments I liked. I scoured magazines, visited decorators' shows, and took notes on ideas I liked in friends' homes. All the while, I became a garage sale and secondhand-store regular.

Now, many years later, I'm so thankful I chose to decorate slowly and realistically. My home isn't perfect, and *Southern Living Magazine* has yet to call and request a photo shoot, but it does beautifully reflect me. It's filled with my favorite colors, unique furniture, and the comforts of home.

Now, as I walk people through our home, I love to share the funny stories of how different items found their way into our rooms. It's been a delightful adventure learning to invite beauty into my home.

Inviting in Peace

To invite peace into a home means to make it the safe haven we all long to escape to, a place where our guards are let down and for better or worse our real selves shine through. Because I'm the mother of six children, peace in our home doesn't necessarily mean it's quiet and without incident. I've learned that while kids are young, peace means having the patience to deal properly with the occasional fight, my favorite trinket getting broken, and the keys to my van mysteriously disappearing. It means realizing that things are replaceable but people aren't.

That's hard to remember when I find my children have done some home decorating of their own. Hope once decided that if she dumped enough powder in her room, she could make it look like heaven. Ashley felt Mommy's bathroom needed more color and texture. She fixed the problem using lipstick, hair gel, and feminine pads that "are like stickers and shaped like little footprints, Mommy." Brooke used the living room walls and windows as marker boards for her make-believe classroom. The boys didn't know that bleaching their tennis shoes in the bathroom could result in their clothing and our blue walls suddenly becoming white polka-dotted.

Sometimes I have a hard time finding the humor in these redecorations, and I feel as though I'll explode if I find one more tube with the toothpaste squeezed out into some unexpected place. I want my kids to act responsibly and to treat our things with care. Those lessons are taught while we clean up each incident. But I also want my kids to know that Mommy loves them more than I dislike the messes. I would never trade them and their imaginations for a peaceful home of perfection that didn't include them.

Peace must be beauty's companion. You can't invite one without the other. Beauty without peace makes for an intimidating home. Kids will be kids, complete with red juice stains and fingerprints galore. Husbands will be men, complete with muddy boots and underwear that never quite makes it to the dirty clothes hamper. Even guests will have the occasional spill and mishap. While we should strive to keep our homes neat and tidy, perfection is unrealistic.

Inviting in Hospitality

I love gingersnap cookies. Their aroma warms my heart, and their taste satisfies my sweet tooth. I remember as a young girl walking in the door from school and smelling ginger floating in the air. The cookies weren't the only thing that made me happy. Gingersnaps meant my mom had thought of me that day and wanted me to feel special. She had taken time out of her busy schedule to tickle my heart.

Recently, my kids and I made the nearly ten-hour drive to visit my family, and guess what delighted my senses when I first opened my parents' front door? All these years later Mom remembered. Her little girl was coming home, so she had pulled out the old recipe and let ginger remind me how much I'm loved.

That's what it means to invite hospitality into our homes. It means making home a place where needs are met and hearts are lovingly touched. To do this you don't have to have magazine-perfect decor or even a lavish banquet of food. We are told in Romans 12:13 to simply, "Share with God's people who are in need. Practice hospitality" (NIV).

Isn't it interesting that "hospitality" is close to the word "hospital," which is where hurting people go to find relief and healing? I think to practice hospitality the way God commands means we must prepare our homes to be places where our family and friends feel relief and healing—relief from this crazy world and healing for all that has been thrown at them that day.

What could you do to tickle the heart of your husband and children today? How could your home be like a spiritual hospital to a hurting friend or neighbor? How could you use the home God has entrusted to you to bring glory and honor to His name?

You now know that you need to invite five guests of honor to your house party: love, tradition, beauty, peace, and hospitality. The specifics of how you pull your party together will express your uniqueness and creativity. Decorate the place to your heart's content!

One other word. We can't leave this chapter without remembering a very precious passage of Scripture. In John 14:2 Jesus says, "In My Father's house are many dwelling places; if it were not so, I would have told you; for I go to prepare a place for you." Jesus is in heaven right now preparing your eternal home. Can't you just see Him making this place with you in mind? Oh, how it must warm His heart to see you do for others what He is doing for you.

TWENTY-ONE

Organizing Your Home

Sharon

I am sure many of you have invited the presence of loveliness into your home, but you just don't know where to find it! So let's clean out the clutter, take an inspection tour, and get organized.

Linda from Alaska wrote the following letter that encourages even those who feel they aren't natural homemakers:

> *I went to work when my kids were small because I couldn't stand being home and I didn't know how to properly run a household. When I was growing up, I was very much into my music and did not learn how to clean, cook, handle money, etc. I was in total shock when I married and had a home of my own. Work was an escape because I am a very organized person and had control and satisfaction at the office, unlike at home.*
>
> *When I moved to Alaska, I had the opportunity to take a class on home organization from a woman who went from slob to totally organized. I discovered that I could run my home a lot like I ran the office, with time management, files, etc. Wow! What a discovery! I actually*

149

began to love caring for my home. Looking back, I would give anything to have known this information when my boys were small. I can plainly see that my life would have taken a different course, including that I probably would not have divorced my first husband.

I guess the bottom line is, please urge women who do not know how to care for their homes, and for whom it is important, to seek help!...It can be learned and it can be enjoyed."[1]

Home is a place where bodies are refueled and souls are recharged. It's a place where we can remove our masks, let down our defenses, and expose our innermost thoughts and feelings. In this crazy game of life, this is the one place where we have the home court advantage. But for many women, home is not a place of quiet rest. It is more like corporate America out of control.

My friend Mary Johnson felt that way. Her homemaking ran in a cycle of neglect-clean-neglect-clean. Then one day she realized she was "servicing her house" instead of making her house a "home that served her." She decided that her resolve of "one day I'm going to get organized" had arrived, and she set out to do just that. Much of the material in the following pages consists of lessons I've gleaned from Mary.

Our world is busier and more complex than it was just a few generations ago. Rarely can we afford the luxury of doing things at a leisurely pace. Instead, most of the time we need to perform tasks efficiently and effectively. Even though the word "organization" conjures up warm and fuzzy feelings about as much as the word "budget," it's key to creating a warm and loving environment for your family and friends.

I've learned that being organized is much like living within the boundaries of God's Word. Neither is meant to constrict us but rather to free us. A well-organized home is one that is thoughtfully and carefully arranged to serve the family's needs.

- It is *not* having everything pin neat and perfectly clean, twenty-four hours a day.

- It *is* having a home that serves your family effectively and meets needs.

- It is *not* making family members walk on eggshells for fear they might get something out of place.

- It *is* teaching the family to take part in making your home an orderly, fun place to live.

- It is *not* something that can be done once and then forgotten about for the rest of your life.

- It *is* something that can be attained and maintained for the rest of your life.

- It is *not* something that everyone loves to do.

- It *is* something that everyone can learn to do and receive a lot of pleasure and satisfaction from.

Having your home in order does wonders to maintain and restore emotional peace when schedules are hectic. You'll be more likely to demonstrate hospitality and invite people in to share God's love. You'll be freed up mentally to be a better listener to your husband and children instead of being preoccupied with a house in disarray. Your home will become a haven for children with hurts and a husband who has had a hectic day at work. So roll up your sleeves and let's get started.

Clutter Control

Perhaps one of the biggest obstacles to having an organized home is clutter. Webster defines *clutter* as "an untidy mess, things left around untidily, a number of different things scattered in disorder."

Clutter is not a disease; it's a symptom. The disease is a lack of workable, practical, and usable placement of things. If your home isn't arranged effectively, you'll know it because you'll have several places where clutter collects—that's the symptom. Whenever clutter exists, something doesn't have a good place to belong.

The Battle Plan

So how do we go about attacking clutter? My toughest area of clutter is paper control. I'm convinced that one reason the Proverbs 31 woman accomplished so much is that she didn't have to deal with junk mail, manuscripts, magazines, newspapers, school papers, and reports. Here are some helpful ideas adapted from *P31 Woman* magazine on what to do with a piece of paper.

- *Answer it:* Respond immediately to letters or invitations. If you don't have time to answer a letter immediately, create a file for letters to be answered.

- *Record it:* Record any important dates and times on a master calendar, and throw the reminder away. Record any addresses in a Rolodex or address book. (I prefer a Rolodex to an address book because addresses become extinct so quickly. It's much neater to throw away a Rolodex card than to scratch out an address in a book. If you do use a book, I suggest writing in pencil.)

- *File it:* Create a filing system of colored folders. File insurance information, bills to be paid, school records, medical records, articles for later reference, etc. Have one set of folders for reference and one for action. (The bill folder would be for action. Records would be for reference.) I have family files in one area and Proverbs 31 files in another.

- *Stop it:* Use a form letter or personal note to ask to be removed from mailing lists. Don't continue receiving something if you don't read or use it. For accuracy, use the peel-off address label on the item's cover to inform the company you wish to have your name removed. To take your name off mailing lists for credit card solicitations, catalogs, and other advertisements, send a postcard to Direct Marketing Association, P.O. Box 9008, Farmingdale, NY 11735, asking that your name be removed from the mail preference service.

- *Pass it on:* If someone can use what you have, pass it on. Consider recycling books, coupons, magazines, newsletters, and catalogs to libraries, waiting rooms, laundromats, paper drives, or the gym.

- *Throw it away:* Once you've answered it, recorded it, filed it, or passed it on, throw away the rest.[2]

Now that we have a plan to deal with paper in the present, let's tackle the clutter from the past. Pick one room in your house that has the most clutter, perhaps a spare bedroom that serves as a storage room. (How did I know that?) Begin with the room itself, and then move to the closets and drawers. Collect three large boxes or opaque trash bags. Label them "throw away," "give away," and "put away." Then grab your three bags and start to pull items out from under the bed, off of shelves, out of the closet, and out of drawers.

> *Throw away:* In the throw away bag, put old magazines, unusable and broken objects, and "I'm going to get around to looking at this one day" reading material. Fill the bag, put a twisty around the top, place it in the garbage, and don't look back!

> *Give away:* In the give away bag, put old but usable clothing, knickknacks that you really don't care for, toys your children have outgrown, items that you haven't used in several years (extra dishes, placemats, jewelry). Give the items to the Salvation Army or to a needy family or store them for a yard sale to earn extra cash.

> *Put away:* In the put away bag, put items that are out of place or don't have a place…yet. In this bag, you may include items that need "recycling," such as half-used notebooks, vintage clothing for playing dress up, old jewelry for little girls, etc. Caution: Don't get carried away in recycling. If it's junk, junk it.

Deal with the throw away and give away items swiftly and with resolve. If you haven't worn something in a couple of years, you probably won't. One reason we have such a hard time deciding what to wear each day is because we have too much unused clothing to choose from. Get tough and get rid of what you don't wear.

Place the put away items in a pile off to the side and get rid of the rest. We'll deal with the put aways in a moment, but just think: Two-thirds of the clutter already is gone! (Realize that the room at hand will be quite messy until the task is complete. Give yourself a month per room.)

Granted, not all the clutter belongs to you. Get family members involved to eliminate their own squirrels' nests.

The Inspection Tour

Now that you've cleared out the clutter and can see the floors and the furniture again, you're ready to organize. You've heard the saying "Everything in its place and a place for everything." Well, if everything is in its place, but you can't get to it easily, it's not in a good place. To get organized, take an inspection tour to see just how well your home is working for you.

Set aside about thirty minutes to one hour on a day when distractions are minimal. Grab a pad of paper and a pen and begin your tour.

Walk in your front door and take notes. What do your guests see when they walk into your home? Is it warm and inviting?

Then go from room to room asking yourself the following questions:

- What is the function of this room? What do we like to do here?

- How can we improve its function and allow it to meet our needs more efficiently?

- Are items in here that we don't need or that belong in another room?

- Are there any areas where clutter consistently piles up? Do those items need a logical place to rest, such as a desk, a clear plastic storage

155

container stowed under the bed, an extra shelf in a closet?

Example: Mary didn't have a desk or worktable in her house. As a result, both of her bedroom nightstands ended up covered with notes, pens, pencils, books, etc. She eventually remodeled her kitchen and had a desk built in. The desk took care of the clutter in other areas.

- Am I seeing anything unsightly that needs to be kept out of view?

  Example: In the kitchen, are Brillo pads, dingy washcloths, or soggy soap bars visible? Consider storing such items in a pretty pottery jar and try to keep all cleaning utensils and products out of sight.

- What do I notice first when I enter the room? What kind of impression does it give? What causes that impression, and what can I do to change it if I don't like it?

  Example: Visitors tend to enter my house through my garage door instead of the warm and inviting front or side porch doors. The garage entrance was always dirty from handprints and filthy tennis shoes. The dog slept at the top of the steps, keeping the wall and door grungy. Instead of trying to teach old dogs (and people) new tricks, I painted the door red with a glossy, washable paint, painted a dog house on the wall where Ginger slept, and placed a cheery chalkboard on the wall to write messages. All this added up to "Welcome!"

Tackling the List

Now that you've eliminated clutter and made a list of changes you would like to make, pick a room you would like to concentrate on. For example, let's pick the den. Once again, start by asking some vital questions.

What do you like to do there? Read, talk, watch TV, listen to music, take naps on the couch, play board games?

- *Read:* Have a comfortable chair with good, soft lighting. Place a basket by the chair for magazines or a coffee table for books to prevent clutter from piling up.

- *Watch TV:* Hide the TV or stereo in a cabinet, if possible. Store videos near the VCR, under cover.

- *Nap:* Place a comfy afghan or quilt over the couch.

- *Play games:* Keep games stored away in a cabinet. In our home, when Steven was young, we kept his toys in an old, refinished cabinet in the den. It was his responsibility to put away his toys each day. Now that we are out of the toy stage, we keep games in the same cabinet. The way you organize a room will change with the changing needs of your family.

After you decide how your family uses the room and what you need to meet those needs, look around and see if any items are superfluous and need to be moved to another area of the house.

Organizing Your Kitchen

Oh, the den is easy, you say, but what about the kitchen? Of all the rooms in the house, the kitchen needs to be the most efficient. One basic rule of thumb for any room, especially the kitchen, is: Give the handiest, prime space only to those items you use on a regular basis.

- Keep items that you use often close to the area in which they are used. Glasses near the sink or refrigerator, pots near the stove, pans near or under the oven, plates near the table, silverware near the plates, cooking utensils near the stove, spices near the stove.

- Keep small appliances, such as the coffee maker and electric can opener on the counter or on a front shelf in the cupboard. If they are on the counter, make sure they are clean and don't detract from the kitchen's appearance.

- Strive to keep as much counter space clear as possible to create an effective workspace.

- Use your highest and lowest cupboard shelves for storage of things you use less often. Put items you rarely use toward the back. If you haven't used something in five years, consider giving or throwing it away.

- Store spices on a lazy Susan or on the shelf in alphabetical order in rows, with the larger items stacked in the back.

- Items you use every day should be within arm's reach. If you need a step stool to get to something daily, move it to a more accessible location.

- Clean out that drawer crammed with loose cooking utensils. Place the cookie cutters in a plastic bag. Throw away unused duplicates. (Do you have six sets of place mats but use only two? Get rid of the other four.) If you have to push other items out of the way to find what you need, there's too much in the drawer. Purchase plastic dividers; place large utensils in a pretty crock.

✍ Cluster canned goods in categories on the shelf: vegetables, fruits, soups, cereals, baking supplies, etc. When restocking supplies, maintain the clusters to locate foods quickly and easily.

I feel like the writer of Hebrews 11:32-33, who began listing the great men and women of the faith. "And what more shall I say? For time will fail me if I tell of Gideon, Barak, Samson, Jephthah, of David and Samuel and the prophets, who by faith conquered kingdoms, performed acts of righteousness, obtained promises..."

What shall I say then, for time will fail me if I speak of organizing the bedroom, bathroom, closets, and garage! But these ideas give you a good start.

Housework

Erma Bombeck said, "Housework is like stringing a strand of pearls with no knot in the end." It's easy to feel that your family is the enemy when it comes to keeping the home clean. They sabotage your efforts by walking on the floor you've just scrubbed and actually wearing the clothes you've just laundered. How dare they!

I was feeling that way one day as I mopped the kitchen floor, when God spoke to my heart. I put down my mop and picked up a pen. This story also appears in my book *Becoming a Woman Who Listens to God,* but it's so apt for the current discussion I had to include it here.

Thank You, Lord, for My Dirty Floor

Do you sometimes get tired of the endless hours of housework? The washing...the ironing...the dusting...the cooking...the washing again. One day mopping the kitchen floor had me in a less-than-cheerful mood. Then I had a thought. Suppose I was blind, and I couldn't see the beautiful patterns on the linoleum floor or the spilled juice by the refrigerator or the crumbs under the baby's chair? If I were deaf, I couldn't hear the soothing sound of the soap bubbles dissolving in my scrub bucket. I couldn't hear the rhythmic sound of the mop being pushed back and forth across the floor's hard surface. Suppose I was in a wheelchair, and I wasn't strong enough to stand upright and grasp the wooden handle to erase the muddy footprints and make the floor shiny and clean again? Suppose I didn't have a home or a family to clean up after?

When I thought about all these blessings, my grumblings turned into a prayer of thanksgiving. "Thank You, Lord, for the privilege of mopping this dirty floor. Thank You for the health and the strength to hold this mop, for the ability to wrap my agile fingers around its handle and feel the wood in my hands. Thank You for the sight to see the crumbs and the dirt, for the sense of smell to enjoy the clean scent of the soap in my bucket. Thank You for the many precious feet that will walk through this room and dirty it up again. Those feet are the reason I do this job. And, Lord, thank You for the privilege of having a floor to mop and a family to clean up after."[3]

It's a Family Affair

Even though the responsibility of creating a warm and loving environment for family and friends falls mainly on the lady of the house, I feel strongly that cleaning is a family affair. I remember one of my son's friends asking, "Why doesn't Steven have splatters all over his mirror?"

"Because," I answered, "he has to clean it up himself so I guess he's careful."

The little friend had a maid. Cleaning up after himself was a novel idea.

Getting children involved in organizing and maintaining their own living space teaches responsibility, creates a feeling of being a necessary part of a team, and lifts some of the burden from Mom.

I've found that my husband is also a tremendous help. However, in the first ten years of our marriage, housework was a source of contention. What I discovered, after many periods of pouting and sessions of sulking, was that Steve honestly didn't see what needed to be done. I love the title of Sandra Aldrich's book, *Men Read Newspapers, Not Minds,* because that's exactly what I wanted Steve to do, read my mind.

In the first years of our marriage, I felt a tremendous burden to keep our home tidy and clean. I particularly struggled on Sunday evenings after a weekend of people traipsing in and out. I wanted Steve to see what needed to be done and *help!*

Many days he would say, "Just tell me what to do, and I'll do it." But that wasn't good enough for me. If he really loved me, he would see what needed to be done and pitch in. Right? Wrong!

I learned that Steve, even though he is much neater and more organized than I am, didn't see what needed to be done to keep the castle clean. If I loved him, I'd let him know when I was overburdened and ask for his help instead of pouting when he didn't do it automatically. Now, after more than twenty years, Steve has learned ways to help.

Some women like to wake up in the morning to the sound of beautiful music coming from their clock radio. I love to wake up to the sound of clinking dishes as Steve takes them from the dishwasher. He also helps by getting clothes out of the dryer when he hears the buzzer sound. I communicated to Steve that he could help me by doing those two chores. He was relieved finally to know how to help instead of being left to figure out what was wrong with his pouty wife.

When it comes to getting your husband to help around the house, remember this maxim, "Ask and ye shall receive. You receive not because you ask not. You ask and do not receive because you whine" (New Jaynes Version).

TWENTY-TWO

Sanctuary

LYSA

*I*f only my college roommate could see me now. She would never think of me as a person who would write ideas to help others be good keepers of the home. Let's just say cleaning, organizing, and other home management duties aren't skills I come by naturally. After all, I went to college for a whole year before I learned sheets were supposed to be washed!

Proverbs 24:3 says, "By wisdom a house is built, and by understanding it is established; and by knowledge the rooms are filled with all precious and pleasant riches." I've spent hours on my knees praying for wisdom, understanding, and knowledge to know how to turn my house into the kind of home that glorifies God. While I don't feel I've mastered the art of homemaking, I've made strides. I love this quote that should give hope to all of us when we feel intimidated by the Martha Stewarts of the world: "Remember, the ark was built by amateurs and the Titanic by professionals."

To be wise builders of our homes, we need to bring prayer and persistence to the task. Prayer will undergird all we do with a strength that can only come from God. And God can give us an eternal perspective. Then washing clothes, cooking meals, organizing, and taking time to establish family traditions become eternally significant blessings rather than mundane tasks. This new perspective will give us the persistence needed to continue being faithful keepers of the homes God has called us to serve in.

I love what Tracy Porter, author of *Returning Home,* says about the difference between a house and a home. "To me, one is an empty canvas; the other a soul-revealing portrait....Home is sanctuary, inspiration, and a living tribute to all of life's shared and personal glories, as well as quiet moments of reappraisal, even sorrow. Home is a reflection of my loves, my spirit, and my soul. It is not merely where I live; it is where my life is."[1] May it be so for each of us homekeepers.

Splashes from John

SHARON

*S*itting by the fourth pool, my attention is drawn to the fourth principle: The Proverbs 31 woman creates a warm and loving environment for her family and friends. John 4 also takes us to a woman's home. This particular home was in disarray.

Once again we find Jesus by the water, only this time it is a well. Jesus had been very busy in Judea and was on His way back to Galilee. One afternoon, He stopped in Samaria, at a well that Jacob from the Old Testament had given to his sons. While Jesus rested, a Samaritan woman came to the well to draw her daily supply of water for her household.

Jesus said to the woman, "Will you give me a drink?" Now, this was a major request—not what He asked for, but that He asked at all. Traditionally, Jewish men didn't speak to Samaritan women—at least not in public.

She rather flippantly responded, "You are a Jew and I am a Samaritan woman. How can you ask me for a drink?" (verse 9 NIV).

As with Nicodemus, Jesus didn't answer her question but made a comment that took the conversation to a deeper level. "If you knew the gift of God, and who it is who says to you, 'Give Me a drink,' you would have asked Him, and He would have given you living water" (verse 10).

Now this threw her off a bit. "Sir, You have nothing to draw with and the well is deep; where then do You get that living water?" (verse 11). In other words, "Excuse me, but You don't even have a bucket. How are You going to get living water?"

Then He answered and said to her, "Everyone who drinks of this water shall thirst again; but whoever drinks of the water that I shall give him shall never thirst; but the water that I shall give him shall become in him a well of water springing up to eternal life" (verses 13-14).

The woman wasn't sure exactly what Jesus was talking about, but the idea of not having to come and draw water every day was pretty appealing. She wanted what He was offering. But there was one little glitch.

He said to her, "Go, call your husband, and come here" (verse 16).

"I have no husband," she replied (verse 17).

Jesus said to her, "You are right when you say you have no husband. The fact is, you have had five husbands, and the man you now have is not your husband. What you have just said is quite true" (verses 17b-18 NIV).

This sounds like something right out of *People* magazine instead of the first century. Jesus, seeing into her soul, made her a bit nervous, and like many who are intimidated with spiritual truth, she dodged the subject. Instead of answering His request, she started to take Him down a rabbit trail of religious issues such as when and where people ought to go to church.

Jesus didn't go down the trail with her but drew her back to discussing a relationship with God. "God is spirit; and those who worship Him must worship in spirit and truth" (verse 24).

Then Jesus told her some incredible news. He was the Messiah. She got so excited that she left her water pot at the well and ran off to tell her family and friends. After a few hours, she brought a large crowd back to the well to meet this man who had told her everything she had ever done.

Jesus ended up staying in Samaria for a few days and many of the townspeople came to know Him as Savior.

When Jesus met the Samaritan woman at the well, her home life was in shambles. But after one encounter with the Messiah, she was on the road to making it a warm and loving environment for her family and friends. Scripture doesn't tell us, but I suspect the crowds gathered at her house to hear Jesus teach. Oh, what a difference it makes in a home when Christ is at the center of our lives.

Faithfully Oversee Time and Money

TWENTY-THREE

Ms. Thrifty

SHARON

*P*rinciple 5: The Proverbs 31 woman is a faithful steward of the time and money God has entrusted to her.

For interview day in our couples' Sunday school class, my husband and I took our turn in the hot seat facing the class and answering a few questions about what made our marriage a success. Our teacher told both of us the questions ahead of time so we wouldn't be caught off guard. However, Steve and I didn't discuss our answers.

I sat with anticipation, perched on my high-back chair (or should I say "pedestal"). I knew Steve's last question and already was feeling myself becoming puffed up by the accolade that would proceed from his lips. The final question was "What is one thing you admire most about Sharon?" I dreamed he would say, "The way the light shines on her silky, chestnut hair" or "That special twinkle in her deep blue eyes."

I held my breath as Judy posed the climactic question. Steve paused…"She's thrifty," he finally answered.

"Thrifty!" I echoed. "You have to be kidding!"

The class broke out in laughter at my disappointment in Steve's answer. Oh, well, not so romantic after all. But I guess he has a point. From the time we were college students holding a yard sale so we could afford a honeymoon until now, over twenty years later, I've enjoyed saving money, searching for bargains, and learning how to be a "do-it-your-self" Proverbs 31 wife. Over the years I've discovered that, with ingenuity, patience, and creativity, you can do much with little.

But Steve went on to say that being thrifty is more than finding good bargains and clipping coupons. We can be thrifty with our words, not wasting them on idle gossip and tearing others down but lavishing praise and encouragement on those around us. We can be thrifty with our energy, not being drained by wasting hours because we're disorganized but frugally planning ahead. We can be thrifty with time, not squandering it on things that don't matter but investing it in things of eternal value.

I guess, when you look at it that way, being "thrifty" isn't such a bad thing after all.

As we look at the fifth principle—the Proverbs 31 woman is a faithful steward of the time and money God has entrusted to her—let's examine what Scripture has to say. And who knows, maybe we'll even find a few coins at the bottom of the pool.

TWENTY-FOUR

Time Wasters, Time Savers

LYSA

I confess, for years I was a poor time manager. I had good intentions but always seemed to be overbooked, stressed out, and running late. While I've improved significantly, old habits die hard, and sometimes I slip back into an overtaxed lifestyle. I've realized that to be a faithful manager of the time God has entrusted to me, I have to be aware of certain potholes in life's road that are significant time wasters. I need to be on the lookout for shortcuts that can save time.

Putting First Things First

Sometimes I become so wrapped up in the urgent needs and demands that seem to come my way every day that I don't stop to carve out time for what really matters. Starting off my day with the Lord is the best time saver I know of because it settles in my heart what my priorities are. When my heart is right and my spiritual ears are open, then the Lord can establish my plans for the day. It never fails that when I'm too busy to put Him first, nothing seems to go smoothly. When I stop and put Him first, I'm aware of His presence and His provision for me throughout the day's activities.

> *Time Waster:* Rushing into the day without spending time with the Lord.

> *Time Saver:* Spending time with God and allowing Him to direct your steps.

Make Lists and Prioritize, Prioritize, Prioritize

Some people are natural-born list makers, and some aren't. I happen to fall into the "are not" category; however, I've disciplined myself to learn to be a list maker and list follower. Each week I write out what needs to be done. Then I prioritize my to-do's and schedule them into my weekly calendar. By prioritizing my list, I make sure the most important items are taken care of first.

> *Time Waster:* Being overwhelmed by all the to-do's floating around in your head.

> *Time Saver:* Listing and prioritizing your to-do's and establishing your week's schedule ahead of time.

Delegate

Nothing is wrong with asking for a little help from other family members. Make others aware of your needs and ask if anyone could fit some of the household to-do's into his or her schedule. Make sure your "helpers" have time to accomplish the tasks and give them deadlines for the jobs' completion.

> *Time Waster:* Trying to do it all yourself and getting frustrated.

> *Time Saver:* Asking for help and crossing off your list what others can do for you.

Call Ahead

Before running your errands, call ahead to make sure the stores have what you're looking for. Obviously I don't mean to do this for every item on your shopping list, but for items you're unsure about, save time by making certain you're going to the right store.

Time Waster: Running all over town looking for an item.

Time Saver: Calling ahead to find the item beforehand.

Work Smarter, Not Harder

Because I work mostly out of my home, my phone is always ringing. So I clean while I talk. I have a cordless phone, which gives me access to every room in my house. While on the phone I unload and reload the dishwasher, do laundry, make beds, sweep, organize drawers, and so on. I have a minicommand post set up by the phone's base in my kitchen where I keep Post-It notes, my calendar, and a phone record log. If I need to jot down some notes while I'm talking, I leave whichever area I'm cleaning and walk to my kitchen.

Time Waster: Talking on the phone.

Time Saver: Cleaning your house while talking on the phone.

Learn to Just Say No

Sometimes the best time saver of all is simply to say no. More activities than you could possibly accomplish will always clamor for your attention. Ask God to help you discern what activities to pursue. Ask yourself if each activity will still allow you to maintain your priorities of God, husband, family, friends, neighborhood, world. Ask yourself your motivation for doing each activity.

Time Waster: Doing activities God never intended you to do.

❧ *Time Saver:* Doing only those things you are truly called by God to do.

Perhaps some of you are still sitting by the fifth pool feeling a little worried about diving in. Maybe that's because, when it comes to time management, more than once you've found yourself in hot water. Well, it's time to jump in, to stop worrying, and to start planning...

Stop Worrying, Start Planning

Matthew 6:31-34 states, "So don't worry at all about having enough food and clothing. Why be like the heathen? For they take pride in all these things and are deeply concerned about them. But your heavenly Father already knows perfectly well that you need them, and he will give them to you if you give him first place in your life and live as he wants you to. So don't be anxious about tomorrow. God will take care of your tomorrow too. Live one day at a time" (TLB). Regarding this Scripture, a marginal note in *The Life Application Bible* offers this advice, "Planning for tomorrow is time well spent; worrying about tomorrow is time wasted. Sometimes it's difficult to tell the difference. Careful planning is thinking ahead about goals, steps, and schedules, and trusting in God's guidance. When done well it can help alleviate worry. The worrier is consumed by fear and finds it difficult to trust God. The worrier lets his plans interfere with his relationship with God. Don't let worries about tomorrow affect your relationship with God today."[1]

I learned that God is intimately concerned about every detail of my life when my second daughter, Ashley, was hospitalized for an extended amount of time as a baby. My natural tendency would have been to fret over how we would pay all the insurance co-pays and extra expenses. However, I was so consumed with praying for her just to live, I knew I had to turn the financial concerns over to the Lord.

Just before Ashley had to be hospitalized, our insurance had changed. I'm not a detail-oriented person so I didn't realize that our new policy covered one hundred percent of our hospital costs. What a relief to discover God had, indeed, taken care of my worry before the problem even existed. In the same way, God considers your every need.

Let me encourage you to move past all the worrying and on to effective praying and planning. I believe the best method for using your time wisely is to develop a plan bathed in prayer and based on Scripture.

One approach to planning that has been helpful to me is to create a life plan, a method that enables me to look at each area of my life and to create priorities for it. In my book *Living Life on Purpose* I listed a step-by-step procedure to help structure each of the seven sections of a life plan. I think you'll find that writing out a life plan will help you not only to get a better handle on your time but also to live every area of your life purposefully.

To start, list each of the principal roles in your life. I wrote down being a child of God, a wife, a mother, a keeper of my home, a faithful steward of the time and money entrusted to me, a friend, and a servant to those in my church and community (based on the seven principles of the Proverbs 31 woman). Under each area I jotted down a plan to help me to keep my priorities straight and my schedule manageable. Here's an overview of how I used the process for time management:

Step 1: Pray

Write out Scripture as a prayer for each area of your life. Why scriptural prayers? Well, we know that when we pray the Word of God we're praying the will of God. God will be faithful to answer prayers that are in accordance with His will. Every area of our lives should be covered in the protection and provision that only the power of prayer can provide.

One of the prayers I wrote was: Lord, You bless me with twenty-four hours in every day. Help me to manage my time well. "You have searched me and you know me. You know when I sit and when I rise; you perceive my thoughts from afar. You discern my going out and my lying down; you are familiar with all my ways" (Psalm 139:1-3 NIV). You assure me that as long as I place my hope in You, Lord, that my strength will be renewed, and I really need renewed strength. I will soar on wings like eagles; I will run and not grow weary; I will walk and not grow faint (Isaiah 40:31).

Step 2: Understand God's Word

Study what God's Word says about each area of your life. Romans 12:2 commands us, "Do not be conformed to this world, but be transformed by the renewing of your mind, that you may prove what the will of God is, that which is good and acceptable and perfect." The only way to be sure you're heading in the right direction is to read God's Word and to let it renew and transform you. Then you won't have to wonder or hope you're making the right decisions; you'll know.

As a result of reading God's Word, I wrote out this part of my plan: Psalm 139:1-3 says that God knows where I am, what I'm doing, and even what I'm thinking at all times. He searches me and knows me very well. Therefore I must ask Him to direct my thoughts to be godly, my steps to go in His direction, and my actions to glorify Him. I must always be humble enough to keep a teachable spirit and willing to change directions when God leads me to do so. Isaiah 40:31 assures me that as long as I trust God with my days, and place my hope solely in Him, He will give me all the strength I need to accomplish those things I need to do and to say no to everything else.

Step 3: Record Key Scriptures

Write down key verses for each area and memorize them. Have you ever read or heard a Scripture passage that stirred your heart? That's God speaking to you, saying, "Pay attention here. I want you to really get this message." When that happens to me, I know I need not only to write the Scripture on paper but also to record it on the tablet of my heart. As you go through God's Word seeking to understand it as it relates to each principal area of your life, record those Scriptures that speak to your heart.

Part of my plan: Memorize Psalm 139:1-3 and Isaiah 40:31.

Step 4: Plan Your Goals

Write out your prayed-through goals for each area. I love that the first two letters of the word "goal" are "go." That's exactly what our goals should do for us, get us going. Our goals should be destinations we want to reach for a better future. They give us something to aim for and to motivate us to press on.

One of the goals I wrote out for myself was to be an organized time manager with a functioning calendar system.

Step 5: Outline Action Steps

Break down each of your goals into practical action steps. If a goal is a destination, then our action steps are like the map marking the road we must travel. These are specific, measurable steps.

My action steps were to:

- Write all scheduled events on my master calendar

- Predetermine what the limit for activities is for each week and say no to anything additional once the limit is reached

- Set up a weekly planning session with my family to discuss events planned for that week and logistics for each

Step 6: Set a Realistic Schedule

Write your action steps in your daily calendar. Now that you know the goals you're aiming for in each area of your life and you know the action steps you need to take, implement them in your daily life. It's not enough just to wish you could meet your goals. If they are to become a reality, it will take discipline to accomplish the necessary action steps day by day.

So I wrote on my calendar the Sunday afternoon weekly planning session our family would have.

Step 7: Examine Your Progress

Find an accountability partner to help keep you on track. We all need cheerleaders, those people who stand on the sidelines of our lives and cheer us on to victory. Ask one of these people to take on the additional responsibility of helping to keep you running on the right track. Share with this person where you feel you're weak and ask her to check on how you're doing on a regular basis. Make sure this is a trusted friend who will ask you the tough questions needed to hold you accountable and someone whom you can open up to.

I asked my husband to hold me accountable to conduct the weekly planning sessions and to say no to activities that exceed my time limits.

You might find it helpful to keep your life plan organized and handy in a three-ring binder. I would also encourage you to discuss developing a life plan with your spouse and ask if he would like to do one for himself. Then you can discuss your individual plans and put some ideas together for a master plan for your family in areas such as raising children, financial planning, and outreach opportunities.

My husband and I went away on a planning weekend, without the children, when we did our first life plans. I must admit, I went into the weekend dreading it but walked away from the time excited about our future. Let me encourage you to stop worrying about your future and start planning.

God's miracles are all around, reminding you that He will take care of you and that He is in control. Your part is to plan effectively so you don't spend so much time worrying.

TWENTY-FIVE

Priority Check

SHARON

*A*s we've lingered at the first four pools, how are your priorities lining up? Are you in the flow of the waterfall, putting God, husband, children, and home in proper perspective, or are you trying to swim upstream because your priorities are out of whack? Are your heart's desires matching up with your time commitments?

Now that we've stepped into this fifth pool, I think we should take time to stop and check priorities. Prioritizing your life isn't an easy task. If it were, we wouldn't be writing a book about it.

Dr. Kevin Leman, in his book *Bonkers,* noted, "Getting your priorities straight and sticking to them is one of the most difficult tasks in life."[1] I heartily agree.

So how do we do it? Remember the antidrug campaign slogan in the 1990s, "Just say no"? I think that's a great place to start.

I can hear some of you who know my schedule saying, "Well, Ms. Proverbs 31, I don't hear you saying no much these days." But actually I have been, and believe me, it's not easy. People get mad at you. They may even say they are "disappointed." (That's always a ticket to a guilt trip. I'd suggest you not go there.) Setting priorities and sticking to them requires much time in prayer, asking God exactly what He wants you to do and when He wants you to do it. That takes us back to the first waterfall, doesn't it? We should always begin there.

Just yesterday I was talking to an overwhelmed friend via e-mail. She told me about how her life was spinning out of control as she served on several different committees at her children's school (the bazaar, the wrapping paper fund raiser, homecoming etc.), sang in the choir, taught Sunday school, participated on the pastor search committee, carted three children from one extracurricular event to the other, and so forth. The previous week, she had been out of the house every single night.

"Cynthia," I wrote, "I want you to write down everything you've done over the past two months. Then take that list and go into your prayer closet and pray. Ask God to show you what items on your list someone else could have done. Yes, I know, another person may not have done it as well as you, but that's OK. Place a mark on the list by things that only you could have done."

She told me she would do this, as soon as she found the time.

Women today are too busy being busy. And much of what we do has no eternal value. Setting priorities and sticking to them requires much time in prayer asking God what He wants you to do and when He wants you to do it.

The Five Question Test

Liz Curtis Higgs, in *Only Angels Can Wing It,* lists five questions she asks herself before she takes on a task.

> ✒ Will this activity matter one week from today? One month? One year?

❧ Is there someone who does this task better than I do, to whom I might delegate it?

❧ Does it satisfy a heart need for me or someone I love very much?

❧ What are the ramifications if I don't do it?

❧ What are the outcomes if I do?[2]

Let me give you an example of how I used those questions in my life. One day a church called and asked me to speak to their women's group on one of my favorite topics, "Giving the Gift of Encouragement." It was a dinner meeting, scheduled on February 4, my son's birthday. So I had to ask myself the questions.

Will celebrating Steven's birthday at dinner matter one week from today? One month? One year? Yes, it would.

Is there someone who could plan the celebration and make him feel special and loved better than I could? No, there's not.

Does it satisfy a heart need for me to say no to the speaking engagement and celebrate his birthday instead? Yes, it does.

What are the ramifications if I don't do it? If I don't speak to the women, they will get another speaker and be blessed by her. If I don't stay home and celebrate Steven's birthday, he may think ministry is more important to me than he is.

What is the outcome if I do it? If I stay home, Steven will feel special and dearly loved.

After evaluating my priorities, I stayed home and gave the gift of encouragement to my son instead of to the women at the church. When turning down opportunities, sometimes they will swing back around at a later time.

Sometimes they won't. The church didn't call back. But guess what? My son did.

One major difference exists between money and time. We can look at our checkbooks, savings accounts, and investments and determine exactly how much money we have. However, we never know how many days we will have to make an eternal impact on our families and our communities. Time is a precious commodity. Let's make sure we're faithful stewards of this priceless gift.

Time vs. Money

Every year I receive a notice from the Department of Motor Vehicles, inviting me to spend a few hours in its office. This letter tells me I need to renew my car license. To RSVP, I have two choices. I can drive forty-five minutes to the DMV, stand in line for two hours with fifty other disgruntled commuters, pay the ever-cheerful DMV employee twenty dollars, receive my renewal sticker, and drive forty-five minutes for the return trip home. Or I can add one dollar to my bill, paying twenty-one dollars instead of twenty, send the letter back, and they will mail the renewal sticker to my home. Now, I don't know about you, but that one dollar saved in the first choice isn't worth the time and frustration spent. As we move into being a faithful steward of our time and money, we must evaluate whether money saved justifies time spent. Most of the time it does. But there is always a balance.

TWENTY-SIX

Who Wants to Talk About Money?

SHARON

I—well, both Lysa and I actually—have a confession to make. As we approached writing about the fifth pool, we didn't exactly dive in with enthusiasm but sat cross-legged on the water's edge. Like two little girls we said, "You go first." "No, you go first." "No, I insist. You go ahead. You jump in, and I'll be right behind you."

It seems no one likes to talk about money. It's not exactly an "inspirational" topic. However, when I started to read about finances in the Bible, I realized at least 2300 verses touched on money and two-thirds of Jesus' parables dealt with finances![1] Then I turned again to look at my noble friend in Proverbs 31 and reminded myself that more than half the verses deal with the making and managing of money. The Proverbs 31 woman was financially savvy and a thrifty investor who understood how to work with her hands, look for bargains, earn a profit, prepare for the future, and discover contentment.

She Was a Do-It-Yourselfer

"She selects wool and flax and works with eager hands" (verse 13 NIV).

One of the best ways to save money is to learn how to be a do-it-yourselfer. Yes, it does take more effort, but as I once heard, "Hard work is the yeast that rises the dough."

When I decided to decorate our bedroom, I set out to do it as beautifully and inexpensively as possible. I selected material, located it in stock, found it at an outlet, and finally waited a few weeks for it to go on sale. Watch how the prices fell on the following chart. (Prices are for twenty-one yards of fabric.)

Source	Cost	Seamstress Labor Cost	Total
Suggested retail	$26/yard=$546	$720	$1266
In-stock price	$12.50/yard=$262.50	$720	$982.50
Outlet price	$8.50/yard=$178.50	$720	$898.50
Outlet sale price	$5.88/yard=$123.50	$720	$843.50
Outlet sale price	$5.88/yard=$123.50	Make it myself	$123.50

I followed the same process for purchasing wallpaper, and the price fell from $857.74 to $233.74. Ultimately, a project that could have cost $2123.74, fell to $357.24 with just a little bargain hunting and willingness to try it myself. Now, I know not everyone can sew, but you're capable of learning how to do a myriad of jobs.

For example, if I'm having a problem with an appliance such as the oven or stove, I've learned to ask appliance repair shops if they have a part. Usually, they will order a part and even guide me in how to replace it. This can save on costly house calls and labor.

When Steve and I were poor married college students, he asked me to cut his hair. It was "shear" terror the first time I snipped his coiffure. It must have taken me close to an hour to finish the job. But, by the time we graduated, I was clipping along at ten minutes a trim. Later, even when he could afford a "professional" haircut, he decided he would rather save the money and the time spent at the barber and have me do it at home. (Just so you know, Steve doesn't cut my hair. I'm thrifty, but not *that* thrifty.)

She Knows the Secret to Contentment

"Her husband has full confidence in her" (verse 11 NIV).

Mary Elizabeth was strolling down the cookie aisle at Wal-Mart with her three-year-old daughter, Sarah, riding comfortably in the "front seat" of the buggy. Suddenly, Sarah spied a box of sugar cookies, coated with pink icing and decorated with multicolored sprinkles.

Her eyes brightened with enthusiasm as she put on her best cherub face. "Mommy, I want those cookies."

"Oh, Sarah," replied her mom, "we don't need any cookies today. We have plenty at home. Maybe another time."

Ten minutes later, as Mary Elizabeth passed through the checkout line, Sarah tried again. "Mommy, I need those cookies."

"No, Sarah, you don't need those cookies. We have plenty at home, and I'm not buying cookies today."

Finally, as they pulled out of the Wal-Mart parking lot, Sarah gave it one last try. "Mommy, I think God wants me to have those cookies."

Cissy, Sarah's grandmother, laughed when she told me this story. I laughed, too. It was kind of a nervous laugh. For just a moment, I saw myself riding through life in a shopping buggy, pointing at first one thing and then another singing, "I want…I need…God wants me to have."

Sarah already had learned our mechanism for justifying materialistic whims. Whether it's sugar cookies with sprinkles on top or a new red convertible, we mere mortals, given enough time, follow that same progression. For Sarah, she went from want to need to God wants me to have in a matter of minutes. For us, it may take a little longer, but the tendency is still there.

In America, the average size of a new home has grown from 1500 square feet to 2190 square feet, and the number of cars has risen from one car for every two Americans to one car for each driving-age individual.[2] The number of cruises taken each year has risen from 500,000 to 6.5 million, and the production of recreational vehicles has risen from 30,300 to 239,300.

Does this mean we're happier and more satisfied? Journalist Kathy Bergen notes, "A growing body of research is reaching the conclusion that the country's unprecedented surge in affluence is not spawning a corresponding surge in contentment, personal or societal."[3]

Robert E. Lane, professor emeritus of political science at Yale University, notes that there's a general "spirit of unhappiness and depression haunting advanced market democracies" (that's us). He goes on to say we're experiencing a rising tide of clinical depression and that Americans are no happier than we were when our incomes were one third of what they are now, back in 1948.[4]

One of the wealthiest men in the Bible, King Solomon, concluded this about the accumulation of wealth as it relates to contentment: "I have seen all the things that are done under the sun; all of them are meaningless, a chasing after the wind" (Ecclesiastes 1:14 NIV). If we are banking on money to bring us happiness, we may find ourselves emotionally bankrupt.

A clear example of the magnetic pull of advertising to create a sense of dissatisfaction was seen in an American company that opened a new plant in Central America because the labor was plentiful and inexpensive.

> Everything was progressing smoothly until the villagers received their first paycheck; afterwards they did not return to work. Several days later, the manager went down to the village chief to determine the cause of this

188

problem, and the chief responded, "Why should we work? We already have everything we need." The plant stood idle for two months until someone came up with the bright idea of sending a mail-order catalogue to every villager—there has never been an employment problem since![5]

Crown Ministries Small Group Financial Study lists three truisms: The more television you watch, the more you spend; the more you look at catalogues and magazines, the more you spend; the more you shop, the more you spend.[6]

Perhaps one reason the Proverbs 31 woman used her time so well and seemed content was that she had no shopping malls and slick media distracting and enticing her.

Psychologists agree that two of our greatest needs are significance and security—for men it's more significance and for women it's more security. However, those needs won't be met at pool five, or at pools four, three or two. Our needs for significance and security can only be met at pool one. There we discover we're significant because we're chosen and dearly loved (Colossians 3:12), children of God (1 John 3:1), and an expression of Christ (Colossians 3:4). We're secure because we're joint heirs with Christ, sharing His inheritance with Him (Romans 8:14-15), have been blessed with every spiritual blessing in the heavenlies, and assured that our God will never leave us or forsake us (Hebrews 13:5).

But wait a minute, you say, doesn't Psalm 37:4 state, "Delight yourself in the LORD; and He will give you the desires of your heart"?

Yes, it does. However, I believe as we spend time by the first pool, fellowshiping with Christ, feeding on His Word, and allowing Him to transform our minds to be like His, our desires transform into His desires. Our longings become conformed into His longings. Therein lies the secret to

189

contentment. "But godliness actually is a means of great gain, when accompanied by contentment" (1 Timothy 6:6). Contentment isn't getting what you want, but wanting what you have.

You may wonder why I coupled a section on contentment with the verse "Her husband has full confidence in her." Studies show that battling over finances is the number one cause for divorce in our country.[7] Husbands and wives argue over finances more than any other subject. And a woman's lack of contentment and her overspending is a flashing neon sign that says to her husband, "I'm not satisfied with how you are providing for me," thus dashing his sense of self-esteem and worth.

Willard Harley, in his book *His Needs, Her Needs,* lists "appreciation" as one of a man's five greatest needs.[8] A lack of contentment on a wife's part chews up that need and spits it out. An abundance of contentment says job well done.

Which brings us back to the most important question we can ask regarding the expenditure of our time and money. What would God want us to do? Under His guidance, our path will be made straight and contentment will journey with us.

Called to Be a Stewardess

When I was a little girl, I always wanted to be a stewardess. You know, those glamorous women who wore cute scarves tied in stylish knots around their necks, showed people how to buckle their seatbelts, pointed to the exit doors, and served sodas and peanuts on airplanes. How disappointed I was when I reached my teen years and realized they weren't called stewardesses any longer but flight attendants.

Well, hope isn't lost. I discovered in Scripture that I can still be a stewardess, but of a different variety. In Scripture,

God has more than two hundred fifty names, one being "Master."⁹ He is the Master of the whole earth, as the psalmist says, "The earth is the LORD's, and all it contains" (Psalm 24:1a). As our Master, He has appointed us to be stewards. The Greek word for steward is *oikonomos,* which translates into "manager, overseer, or supervisor." In biblical times, a steward was the supreme authority under the master and had full responsibility for all the master's possessions and household affairs.¹⁰

For us today, God has asked us to be faithful with the resources we've been given, whether that's a little or a lot. (See 1 Corinthians 4:2; Matthew 25:14-23.) As Hudson Taylor said, "Small things are small things, but faithfulness with a small thing is a big thing."

If we waste our resources, the Lord may remove us as steward and look for someone else to fill the position. "There was a certain rich man who had a steward, and this steward was reported to him as squandering his possessions. And he called him and said to him, 'What is this I hear about you? Give an account of your stewardship, for you can no longer be steward'" (Luke 16:1-2). Stewardship is a great responsibility, be it large or small. Someone once said, "It's not what I would do if one million dollars were my lot; it's what I am doing with the ten dollars I've got."

So, you see, we all have the chance to be stewardesses. I don't know about you, but I want to be a good one.

TWENTY-SEVEN

Debt and Giving: Heart Matters

LYSA

*B*efore I married Mr. Budget-Plan-Save, I wasn't much of a financial steward. Money seemed to burn a hole in my pocket. I couldn't wait to spend all I had and then some. It made me feel good to go to the mall and buy whatever my heart desired. Of course, I balanced this with buying for others. I figured in some strange way that would make my runaway spending OK. After all, aren't we supposed to do unto others as we do unto ourselves?

Before long a big black cloud called "debt" hovered over me. It rained on my conscience and overshadowed every aspect of my life. That's about the point when I prayed that God would send someone into my life to teach me how to be a better money manager. God was faithful and sent me a husband who is a financial wiz. He showed me how to balance my accounts and instructed me to make the necessary sacrifices to become debt free. It was hard, incredibly hard, but I did it.

In the process, I learned that I needed to budget and plan for the future. I also learned that just because you have checks in your checkbook doesn't mean you have money in your account.

Probably the most important thing I learned, though, was that my problems with money were just a symptom of a much deeper heart problem. You see, I was seeking satisfaction from money. Sure, my trips to the mall provided a temporary happiness, but it carried the high price of going further and further into debt. I realized I needed something to quench my insatiable thirst and fill that deep longing in my soul. No car, outfit, home, or anything else material could ever do this.

Satisfaction

Do you remember the Samaritan woman at the well we talked about in Section 4? I want to revisit her for just a minute. In John 4:10 Jesus calls Himself the "living water." Why? Because this woman was thirsty, really thirsty, not just for physical water but for something to be poured into her soul to fill her up. For years she had looked for her needs to be met by a man. We know from verse 18 she had five husbands and was living with a man who wasn't her husband. She had an insatiable thirst and spent her life looking in all the wrong places to have it satisfied. Finally, she realized Jesus could fill her longing. In verses 28 and 29 we see something that's beautiful but easy to miss. "So the woman left her waterpot, and went into the city and said to the men, 'Come, see a man who told me all the things that I have done; this is not the Christ, is it?'" Did you catch that? She left her water jar. She had gone to the well to have her physical needs met but forgot all about that when she met Jesus—the living water.

When I examined my heart, I realized I was like the Samaritan woman; I was using money to try to fill the emptiness in my soul. I think that's the cause of debt for many people.

Maybe you thought this section on debt would be filled with instruction on getting out of debt. Well, other books and Bible studies can help you with that. (For more information contact Crown Financial Ministry at 1-800-722-1976.)

I want to tug at your heart and encourage you to find places in your soul that are thirsty, places that demand satisfaction but which you've tried to fill with the quick fix of spending beyond your means, the little nooks and crannies that cry out for more and more. Nothing of this world can fill those soul longings and cravings.

Whatever we seek out to fill us will ultimately be our master. Jesus warned us in Matthew 6:24, "No one can serve two masters; for either he will hate the one and love the other, or he will hold to one and despise the other. You cannot serve God and [money]." God Himself has placed your deep soul longings within you to draw your attention to the eternal realm. He is waiting to pour out His living water, but first you must surrender trying to fill this emptiness yourself. Open your heart, and ask for a drink. In doing so, you'll be satisfied, not because of what you can purchase, but because of what Jesus Christ has purchased for you.

Giving

I always wondered why money was called "dough." Maybe it's from Ecclesiastes 11:1, "Cast your bread on the surface of the waters, for you will find it after many days." What this strange verse is telling us is to give to those in need even though it may seem thrown away or lost, and God will make sure it doesn't sink. When we're willing to give freely, God will see our faithfulness and trust us with more.

Haven't you heard the old saying "You can't outgive God"? How true this is when our giving is done with the right heart attitude. If we view giving as something that takes away from what we want, then we'll never experience joy in giving. But, if we view our giving as a kingdom investment, our whole perspective changes.

I love Matthew 6:19. "Do not lay up for yourselves treasures upon earth, where moth and rust destroy, and where thieves break in and steal; but lay up for yourselves treasures in heaven, where neither moth nor rust destroys, and where thieves do not break in or steal; for where your treasure is, there will your heart be also." Jesus is calling us to check our hearts, to ask whether they are set on eternity or on the here and now.

Winston Churchill said, "You make a living by what you get. You make a life by what you give." If I might take the liberty to tweak his quote a bit, I would say, "You make a living by what you get. You make an eternally significant life by giving for Christ's sake."

A man I know who lives this out is Danny, who has determined how much his family needs for simple yet comfortable living. If his monthly income exceeds this predetermined amount, he gives away the excess. He sees his money as one hundred percent God's, not just ten percent or even a generous fifteen percent. Danny truly believes that God owns it all, and he simply is required to manage his money as if God were the one writing the checks. He knows what it means to be a kingdom investor. Proverbs 28:20 is certainly true in his life, "A faithful man will abound with blessings, but he who makes haste to be rich will not go unpunished."

Being debt free is a heart issue for many of us and so is our giving. Do you have any heart adjustments you need to make?

TWENTY-EIGHT

A Few Coins

LYSA

*S*ometimes a simple story can touch our hearts and teach us more about life than all the instruction in the world. The following recollection, written by my dear friend Mike Griffin, stirred my heart and made me realize God wants us to hold the things of this world loosely and always be willing to let go when the Master calls us to.

Mike writes:

I remember that hot August day in 1961. My cousins, my sister, and I spent most of the summer at our grandparents' house. There were six of us in all, ranging in age from about three to ten. Our parents would leave us with Grandma while they went to their jobs during the day. My grandparents didn't have much, but we never really knew the difference. To us, our grandparents' house was a wonderful place where we were loved and accepted and cared for, albeit quite simply.

And we thought that old house on 22nd Street was a magical place. It had an old basement where we could play Hide-and-Go-Seek, an enormous tree that was perfect for climbing, and a large grassy field where we played baseball. What more could a kid want?

Air conditioning was experienced only in the large department stores or during the occasional adventure to the movie theater. It was hot, and the heat was something that on those summer days could drain even six energetic kids.

As we lolled about the house, a tapping at the screen door rattled the stillness. It might be a door-to-door salesman! In those days salesmen carried large suitcases filled with brushes or pots and pans or some other new gadget. We all knew our grandma had no money to buy the stuff they were selling, but it was fun to watch the man pull out all those neat brushes and brooms and show how they could "clean up the house in half the time." On very rare occasions, that tap at the door might be an uncle or an aunt who had a car and was offering to take us to get ice cream.

We all raced to the door. None of us was prepared for what we saw. A little woman was standing there. We were just kids, but we could tell by looking at her that she had seen hard times, very hard times. Her face was wrinkled, and her shoulders were hunched over. I remember most of all the expression on her face and in her eyes. It was as if she didn't want to see anymore. Even at the age of nine, I knew that to be the look of hopelessness. Her simple dress was patched and frayed. Her shoes had holes.

Behind her stood a little girl, maybe six or seven years old. She was dirty from following her mother about those hot streets. She had no shoes. She had no smile. I remember her hair being matted to her forehead by the sweat, which made little brown lines as it dripped through the dust on her face.

"Is your mother home?" the little lady asked in a weary voice.

"No, but my grandma is," replied my cousin and off she ran to find Grandma.

The rest of us stood there at the door staring. We said nothing. We all wanted to do something, but we didn't know what to do.

Grandma soon hurried to the door, drying her wet hands in her apron as she walked. She pushed open the screen door and peered through her bifocal glasses at our visitors. Before Grandma could speak, the little lady reached into a brown paper bag and pulled out a red foil package. She opened the foil pouch revealing sewing pins and needles.

"Would you like to buy some pins?" she asked.

Grandma, somewhat surprised, her eyesight not the best, squinted to get a better look at the little girl and finally replied, "How much are they?"

The lady replied, "Oh, anything you can give me."

Now, we knew Grandma had no money. It took all of Grandpa's hard-earned paycheck just to cover the bills and buy the groceries. She went to the closet, and we all followed, wondering what she would do.

We watched her pull out her big, black, Sunday pocketbook. She dug in every little pouch and pocket and turned it upside down and shook it. She found one dime and two pennies in a crease in the bottom. Going back to the kitchen, she pulled out a large brown paper grocery bag. She filled it up with cans of tomato soup, potatoes, tomatoes, and beans from her garden, and biscuits she had made for supper.

She tucked a doll into the bag, carefully hiding the toy beneath the food. She had kept the doll, which had belonged to one of her children, on the mantel above the fireplace. And she had made a beautiful dress for it with leftover pieces of material from her sewing projects. We knew this doll was special to her; none of the girls ever played with "Grandma's doll."

Grandma went back to the front door and gave the lady the bag of groceries and the twelve cents. She said, "This is all I have. Please take it, but please don't make me take your pins."

"Thank you, ma'am," said the lady, barely able to speak. She turned and walked down the blistering street with the little girl silently following, but we barely saw them. We kids were watching our grandmother. We knew when she had her eyes closed and her mouth was moving quietly that she was praying. She acted as if she were watching the little family walk down the hill, but we knew she was praying for them.

We were in awe of our grandmother. Even at our young age, we knew we had witnessed what Jesus had said, "She has given more than all the others. She has given all she had."

Splashes from John

The fifth principle states that the Proverbs 31 woman is a faithful steward of the time and money God has entrusted to her. As we sit by the fifth pool, focusing on the fifth principle, the fifth chapter of John draws our attention to another fellow sitting by a pool, too.

In Jerusalem, one of the places where people met was called the sheep gate pool. Surrounding the pool were five porticoes, or shelters, where people with various illnesses clustered, waiting for the "moving of the waters." They believed an angel of the Lord came down at certain seasons and stirred the pool. When the people saw the waters ripple, they all made a mad dash to jump in. The first one in was healed from whatever disease he had.

One man had been lounging by the pool for thirty-eight years. Talk about not being a faithful steward of time and money; he had wasted thirty-eight years of his life. However, as with many who find themselves in an unproductive situation, he blamed his lot on other people.

Jesus walked up to the man and asked, "Do you wish to get well?"

To some that might seem like an unusual question. To others, it's a poignant conviction. Sometimes we get so used to our troubles and so comfortable with our discomfort, that we don't really want to get well. Since I've counseled countless women, advising them on how to change their situations and watching them continue in the same muck and mire, Jesus' question doesn't surprise me.

The sick man answered, "Yes, I'd like to get well, but there's nobody to help me get in the pool. When the water is stirred, someone always beats me to it."

Jesus doesn't want us to be wasteful. He wants us to invest our talents, whether it be time or money, into others' lives. He certainly doesn't want us to sit by the pool and make excuses.

He turned to the man and said, "Arise, take up your pallet, and walk" (verse 8).

Immediately the man became well, took up his pallet, and began to walk.

Are you lollygagging, dawdling, and dillydallying with one of your most precious commodities—your time? Are you sunk in your sorrows, paralyzed in your pity, or detained by depression? Don't waste another minute expecting a human being to come along and lift you up. Jesus says to you, just as he said to the man by the pool, "Get up and get going!" He is all you need.

PRINCIPLE #6

Mentor Others, Develop Godly Friendships

TWENTY-NINE

Building Relationships

LYSA

*P*rinciple 6: The Proverbs 31 woman speaks with wisdom and faithful instruction as she mentors and supports other women and develops godly friendships.

A carpenter who was known for his beautiful craftsmanship spent his life building exquisite homes. He paid great attention to the details of his work. When it came time for him to retire, his boss asked if he would build one last home as a special favor.

The carpenter reluctantly agreed. Never had his tired hands ached so as once again he sawed and hammered. His heart was no longer in his job. He rushed through his work, using inferior materials and paying little attention to detail. *No one will probably even notice,* he reasoned. He just wanted to finish the job and get on with enjoying his retirement.

Finally the house was completed. But his boss had one last request—for the carpenter to meet him at the house to sign some final papers. When they met, the boss shocked the carpenter by handing him the keys to the house, his retirement gift. Oh, if only he had known, he would have done his best work.

So it is with us. Every day we choose our lumber and nails, as we build our lives. If we build wisely, we establish friendships and mentoring relationships that will endure. However, if we use haphazard methods and just enough effort to make do, we'll never experience the full richness of those relationships. God created us to need others, especially other women, who understand the pulls and strains of trying to be godly wives, mothers, and friends. And God created us to give to others from the knowledge and insights He has provided us. Such a gift is highly personal and greatly prized.

One day our Master Carpenter will ask to meet with us. He'll hand us the keys to the eternal home we've built. Will the structure be strong and solid from years of building into others' lives? Will there be timbers of generosity and nails of love that hold up our structure?

Let's not be disappointed with the structure we've built, with the lives we've lived. Make the investment today to befriend someone and to mentor someone else. Then, when we pick up the keys to our eternal home, we'll hear the Master Carpenter say, "Well done, my faithful servant. You have built well and wisely."

THIRTY

Who, Me, a Mentor?

SHARON

I was sitting in a cross-generational discussion group about the need for mentoring among Christian women when a lady in her twenties expressed how desperately her peers needed older women to come alongside them and share from their experiences as wives, mothers, and friends. I nodded my head in agreement as if to say, "Yes, yes, we do." Then came the shocking realization that she was looking at me, not as a peer who needed mentoring, but as the older woman who needed to do the mentoring.

After I recovered from the initial shock of being considered an "older woman" (I was thirty-nine at the time), I started to think seriously about Titus 2:3-4. "Likewise, teach the older women to be reverent in the way they live, not to be slanderers or addicted to much wine, but to teach what is good. Then they can train the younger women to love their husbands and children, to be self-controlled and pure, to be busy at home, to be kind, and to be subject to their husbands, so that no one will malign the word of God" (NIV).

I asked myself a few questions: What is a mentor? What exactly is a mentor supposed to do? What does the Bible have to say about mentors? Who can become a mentor? How old is older?

What Is a Mentor?

Have you ever driven down a country road when the fog was so thick you couldn't see ten feet in front of you? It can be a terrifying experience. But if another car pulls out in front of you, and you can follow its taillights, suddenly driving in the fog isn't so scary.

I think that's a beautiful picture of a mentor. She is like a light, guiding a fellow traveler down the sometimes foggy, rocky, or bumpy road of life. Speaker Win Couchman described it this way, "A mentor is someone further down the road than you, who is going where you want to go, and who is willing to help you get there."[1] Webster calls her "an experienced and trusted friend and advisor."

Did you notice that neither Titus 2 nor Webster said she had to be an expert or an authority? That should be a relief to us all.

Susan Hunt, author of *Spiritual Mothering,* describes mentoring this way:

> Spiritual mothering [mentoring] is to be impressed on younger women as you prepare the fellowship supper together at church, as you make blankets for the home for unwed mothers, as you sort clothes for the homeless shelter, as you talk about how to maintain a devotional life with three preschoolers competing for your attention, as you walk through the factory making deliveries or into the courtroom to defend a client. Spiritual mothering has more to do with demonstrating

"the shape of godliness" than with teaching lesson plans.[2]

Spiritual mothering takes place when…

A woman possessing faith and spiritual maturity enters into a nurturing relationship with a younger woman in order to encourage and equip her to live for God's glory.[3]

As you can see, mentoring and discipleship go hand in hand; however, whereas discipleship teaches one how to understand God's Word and pray, mentoring demonstrates how to live life.

A Biblical Example of Mentoring

The Bible is full of mentoring examples: Elijah mentored Elisha, Moses mentored Joshua, Jesus mentored the disciples, Priscilla and Aquila mentored Apollos. But perhaps one of my favorite mentoring couplets is Elizabeth and Mary.

In Luke 1, the angel Gabriel delivered to young Mary some pretty incredible news. While still a virgin, she was going to conceive a child by the Holy Spirit and give birth to the Savior of the world. Before Mary could catch her breath, the angel continued by telling her, "Oh, by the way, your supposedly barren cousin, Elizabeth, is also pregnant with child in her old age" (Jaynes version).

God knew that Mary was going to need a mentor and a friend to counsel, comfort, and coach her for the next few months. Our precious Lord created women to desire to be in relationship with each other, and He provided for Mary before she even asked.

So Mary, probably around sixteen years old, traveled one hundred miles from Galilee to Judea to spend three months with her mentor, Elizabeth. When Mary walked into Elizabeth's home, the older woman blessed her. "Blessed are you among women, and blessed is the child you will bear! But why am I so favored, that the mother of my Lord should come to me? As soon as the sound of your greeting reached my ears, the baby in my womb leaped for joy. Blessed is she who has believed that what the Lord has said to her will be accomplished!" (1:42-45 NIV).

Did you notice how Elizabeth confirmed Mary? Can you imagine the jeers and ridicule that Mary anticipated for the months to come? Can you imagine how relieved Mary must have felt to hear those positive words from her mentor?

I can just picture Elizabeth and Mary for the next three months: washing clothes, talking about what to expect during the first two trimesters of pregnancy, baking bread, poring over the ancient scrolls from Zacharias's private library, and discussing how they fit into the prophecies. Certainly Mary helped Elizabeth during the delivery of her son, John. This hands-on experience no doubt proved invaluable as Mary and Joseph delivered their own baby boy in a stable without the help of a midwife.

Elizabeth and Mary were definitely on the same path in life. They both had unusual pregnancies, they both had unusual sons, and they both lost their sons to cruel deaths at an early age. I'm sure, as Mary traveled down her dark and foggy road, her mentor, who had traveled the path before her, helped to light the way. God prepared Mary for what was ahead by providing her a sensitive mentor.

Often God will send someone our way who is going through a struggle that we've already experienced. Scripture says, "Blessed be the God...who comforts us in all our affliction so that we may be able to comfort those who are in any affliction with the comfort with which we ourselves are comforted by God" (2 Corinthians 1:3-4). In other words, God doesn't comfort us to make us comfortable. He comforts us to make us comfortable.

What Is a Mentor Supposed to Do?

Cheryl Gunderson is one of my mentoring heroes. I've watched as she has taken budding adolescents and nurtured them into blooming adults. I asked Cheryl to explain what occurs in her mentoring groups. She told me:

"I gather a group of girls, usually when they are in the ninth grade. Actually, each year, I've felt that God chose the girls and placed them in my arms. Then, for the next four years, I pour my life into theirs. We meet once a week for Bible study and prayer, but I do more than become a part of their week. I become part of their lives. We go shopping, take beach trips, go out to dinner, and have sleepovers at my house. Yes, I become their friend, but they know at the end of each week, I'm going to ask them tough questions like, 'How much time did you spend alone with the Lord this week?' 'How did you apply what we learned from the Bible study to your life this week?'"

One vital part of Cheryl's mentoring is the junior year beach trip. During this weekend, Cheryl discusses with the girls the nitty-gritty of dating, marriage, and how boys view relationships. She talks about body language, such as how sitting in a boy's lap can stimulate him sexually, about how movies affect men's and women's thoughts differently, and about the dangers of intimacy before marriage. These insights always raise a chorus of "Really?" "You've got to be kidding," "I would never have thought about that," and "They're thinking that!?"

But the best part of the weekend is making "The List." Cheryl talks with the girls about what they desire in a godly husband, and each girl makes a list of uncompromisable qualities. The list begins as words on paper but becomes a hedge of protection from the wrong mate and wrong relationships and an encouragement toward the right mate and right relationships. After the girls make their lists, they commit to hold each other accountable through the years and to attend each other's weddings.

Cindy Ely was a part of one of Cheryl's mentoring groups. "I was in Cheryl's group for five years," she said, "and even though I had a close relationship with my mom, I needed someone to talk to who wasn't my mom. Sometimes Cheryl would say the same things my mother said, but I could just receive it better coming from her. I felt I could be honest with Cheryl and she wasn't going to get mad at me or judge me. She was comfortable talking about every aspect of our lives. I think every girl needs another adult female role model besides her mom to encourage her in her walk with the Lord. It made all the difference in the world to me."

I was curious how the mothers of the girls felt about having another woman, close to their own age, so intimately involved in their daughters' lives. Cindy's mom, Grace, said, "When Cindy was in high school, she had constant health problems that affected her physically, socially, and spiritually. Her time with Cheryl gave her confidence, companionship, discipline, and direction. Today, Cindy is a wonderful person with high standards. I always tell Cheryl she partnered with me in raising my child."

Elizabeth Dyar, another of the girls in Cheryl's group, observed, "She has opened herself up and made herself vulnerable to us. I like that because I feel it's then my turn to encourage her, the same way she encourages me."

I want to encourage you. I know Cheryl, and she isn't an unusual, sainted woman who possesses magical keys to unlock the treasures in a teenage girl's heart. She doesn't hold a degree in adolescent behavioral psychology or counseling. She is just like you and me. She is a woman farther down the road than they are, who is going where they want to go, and is willing to help them get there. As Christian mentors, we don't have to have all the answers. We simply need to love and point the way to the Savior who does.

A Mentoring Model for Young Wives and Mothers

Mary Marshall Young has been a mentor for more than twenty-five years. Now in her eighties, she still meets with women on a regular basis and leads them to the throne of grace in God's Word and in prayer. She also offers practical advice to harried mothers and wives.

Mary Marshall said:

> I remember days, as a new mother, when the kids would go off to school, I would go into my bedroom, shut the door, and not come out until they came home. I was so distraught trying to juggle my responsibilities, cope with the suffocating pressures, and raise three children. I just wanted to shut out the world. I went into marriage deeply wounded from a dysfunctional home filled with lots of pain and insecurities, and I had no one to take my hand and guide me in the way I should go. Then one day I cried out to the Lord for help. He took my hand, and I've been clinging to it ever since.

After Mary Marshall's children were grown, God led her to mentor young women. Sometimes she focused on Bible study and prayer. Other times, she suggested practical helps. But she always prayed for the Holy Spirit to reveal to her what each woman needed.

She recalled a couple of women she mentored:

> I remember one very serious, solemn young gal. I felt that she needed to loosen up and have some fun. [Remember, Mary Marshall is eighty.]

So I asked her, "What would you like to do for fun, if you could?" She answered, "Play tennis." So I told her, "Go do it! And if it's rainy outside, go and get you some good movies to watch." See, God showed me that this young lady needed to have some fun and get the focus off herself—plain and simple.

I remember another young lady whose kids ran her ragged. I asked her, "What's the worst time of the day for you?" Without hesitation she answered, "Four o'clock! That's when the kids get wild." So I told her to get the children involved in some activity at home every day at four and spend some quiet time with the Lord by herself. That one little suggestion gave her the oomph she needed for the rest of the evening.

Ann was in her forties and longed for the wisdom of a godly mentor. She struggled with balancing two loves in her life—being a mother to her son and pursuing a challenging career. So she made an appointment to meet with Mary Marshall once a week, beginning in November. Little did Ann know, but her world was about to be rocked on its axis.

When that crisp autumn day arrived, Ann dressed for work, and dropped off her son at school. She wondered what she and Mary Marshall would talk about but knew God was in control. As it turned out, that day Ann's boss walked into her office and stated that her services were no longer needed. Ann drove to Mary Marshall's home a wounded soul who needed to feel the loving arms of her heavenly Father. That's exactly what she received, but the arms looked amazingly like her mentor's.

"I was devastated," Ann said. "But that was only the beginning. A few days later, I found out I was pregnant. Not that being pregnant wasn't a blessing, but being forty and pregnant wasn't in my plans. Then I had another loss as my father died suddenly from a heart attack. My time with Mary Marshall was so providential. It wasn't a counseling session but a healing session. The Lord was orchestrating circumstances of my life to strip away layers of my old sinful nature, and He used Mary Marshall to apply the healing balm of Jesus Christ. As I look back on it now, it was definitely one of the sweetest times of my life."

Of course, neither Ann nor Mary Marshall knew what would occur the very day their mentoring was to begin. But God knew all along. He is Jehovah Jireh, God our Provider. As we've seen with Elizabeth, Cheryl, and Mary Marshall, sometimes He provides through the welcoming arms, tender hearts, and caring words of a mentor.

Mary Marshall told me, "Mentoring is very simple. It just takes time and a willingness to share in someone's life. One thing's for sure: I'm no expert, and I don't have all the answers. But I do know the One who does, and He leads us into all truth."

Mentoring Varieties

Mentoring comes in all shapes, sizes and varieties. Instead of one-to-one mentoring, Betty Huizenga has developed a mentoring program that involves seven women sharing the responsibilities in a six-week class called Apples of Gold. Six of the mentors each teach one lesson from Titus 2: on kindness, loving your husband, loving your children, submission, purity, and hospitality. The seventh mentor is the cooking teacher.

The classes consist of ten to fourteen young women who gather in someone's home for the six sessions. Each session begins with forty-five minutes of cooking instruction, followed by a Bible study lesson. The mentoring continues during lunch with table-talk questions.

Proverbs 31 Ministries is, in reality, a mentoring ministry. Though women don't come to our homes, we go to theirs daily through our radio segments and monthly through our publication, *P31 Woman*. (See ordering information in the appendix.) We realize that sometimes mentors are hard to find. Churches separate congregants according to age and life stage, Grandma's house is no longer "over the river and through the woods," and neighbors often are strangers. Seeing this need, Proverbs 31 Ministries was born. And we know we're serving as mentors by the letters we receive. Here's one of them:

Dear Proverbs 31:

My husband and I separated May 1998. As anyone could imagine, this was an extremely difficult time for our family. My husband moved and I was now home alone with three small children and unemployed. I was devastated. My days were filled with confusion and anger. My focus was on my husband and wondering how could he do this to us...

Fortunately, I had my faith. I turned to God for strength, comfort, and provision. I turned to Him to change my husband.

During a Bible study one Sunday night, a friend asked me if I had heard of Proverbs 31 Ministries. I had heard them on the radio but didn't know they had a monthly newsletter. The following week, my friend brought me some copies. She continued this each time she received a new newsletter. I enjoyed reading the articles on children, organization, housework, and the Scripture study. To be honest, though, I found it difficult to read any article on "A Great Marriage" or "How to Be a Godly Wife." After all, what did I need that for?...

I kept The Proverbs 31 Woman with me alongside my Bible. I would read and reread it often. I clipped the Bible verses and poems that were presented so nicely and put them around my house and van where I could be reminded of God's Word when I would forget or grow weary. I used the Scripture study for daily readings. At times, when I was able to push my anger aside, I began to read the articles on marriage and how to be a godly wife. Something very surprising began to happen.

God began (and continues!) to show me what a godly woman, wife, and mother was through the entourage of articles…He began to drop the scales from my eyes and showed me what kind of woman and wife I was. By the world's standards, I was fine. By God's standards, I was a wretch.

Over the next few months I eagerly read all the articles on marriage and family. The ministry acted as a sort of mentor for me. It gave me biblically based answers to practical questions and problems. I began to pray fervently for my husband and my marriage. And all the while God was giving me the answer to my prayer to change my husband. His answer: He changed me!…

During our separation things went from bad to worse. We ended up in court. I gazed at my husband from across the courtroom and knew this was wrong, very wrong…That night I called my husband and asked him to come home. He was shocked. I told him to the world it was ridiculous, but to God it was simple obedience to Him. My husband came home, and our family was together again…

In a day when we are so busy with schedules, choir, Bible study, children, soccer, lessons of all sorts, housework, work, the myriad of information the media pour before us, it's difficult to cultivate necessary relationships. Relationships with God, family, friends, mentors. I was especially lacking mentors. The Proverbs 31 Newsletter passes to us invaluable life lessons from others that have gone before us that we need to mature...

I include this letter, not as an ad for our ministry, but for you to get a taste of how desperately the world needs godly mentors.

Who Can Be a Mentor?

We all can be mentors. Chances are, if you're reading this book, you know women who are younger than you who could benefit from your life experiences. Chances are, if you're reading this book, you know women who are older than you from whom you can draw a wellspring of knowledge. Your life experiences are much like the treasures or talents mentioned in Matthew 18. Let's not bury those treasures but invest them in others.

THIRTY-ONE

The ABCs
of Friendship

LYSA

riendship is all about give and take. I've catego-
rized what makes friendships great by working my
way through the alphabet. So come along with
me as we journey our way through the A–Zs of friendship.

Accept Each Other

One of our most basic needs is to be accepted by others. So it just makes sense that this need would be met
through friendships, right? I know firsthand what it's like
to have friends who love and accept me just as I am. But I
also know what it's like to have friends who are determined
to change or "fix" me. Nothing can damage a friendship
faster than being made to feel unaccepted.

If you think something needs to change in your friend,
ask the Lord to either change your friend or to change your
heart. If you feel that you need to confront your friend about
a specific issue, use words that will help and not hurt. Stay
focused on the issue at hand and never condemn her as a
person. Avoid using definitive statements such as "you
never" and "every time." Remember, loving accountability
has a place in friendships, but acceptance must come first.

Believe in Each Other

When I was in high school, I was involved in the choral program. We were a bunch of kids who loved to sing, and some of us even had talent to offer our kind and patient choral director, Dr. Byron Smith. His wife, Bobbie, was the pianist, and together they helped us sound pretty good, I must say. We even won some regional and state competitions.

Students in the choral program weren't the most popular kids or the coolest, but we shared a special bond. Dr. Smith believed in us and taught us that believing in each other could transform our group.

I've never forgotten what Dr. Smith taught, and today I'm committed to encouraging others to discover all that God intends them to be. Too many people give up on life dreams because they aren't encouraged to pursue them. What might your friends accomplish if you let them know you believe in them?

Cry with Each Other

A crowd of friends sat quietly talking and praying with my husband and me as we waited in the intensive care waiting room for news of our daughter Ashley. We had been told a few hours earlier that the doctors weren't sure if she would make it through the night. The pain at hearing those words was almost unbearable.

But my friends were there, and though they spoke few words, their tears comforted me. Their tears told me they loved our six-week-old daughter and felt our pain at possibly losing her.

Sometimes when friends go through crises, we feel we need great words of biblical wisdom to share. In reality our tears may bring the greatest comfort. Romans 12:15 says, "Rejoice with those who rejoice, and weep with those who weep." I'm so thankful I had friends who did just that. They wept with us in our time of grief and rejoiced with us when God spared our precious little one.

Defend Each Other

Satan loves to make God's beloved children forget their position in Christ and feel shame and condemnation. It's so easy to listen to Satan's deceptive whispers and to believe his lies that we are worthless and unimportant. Oh, how vital it is that we have a friend to remind us of our position as holy and dearly loved children of the King. We all need a friend who reminds us to seek the truth that dispels the lies and then gets down on her knees to pray for us. Will your friends stand in the gap to defend you and to pray for you? If not, ask God to send you such a friend.

In the Bible we see a beautiful picture of this in David and Jonathan's friendship. Jonathan's father, King Saul, wanted to kill David. Jonathan not only defended David by protecting him from Saul's destructive plans but also swore that a love would exist between their descendants forever (1 Samuel 20:42).

Exemplify Jesus in Relating to Each Other

Many years after Jonathan saved David's life, Jonathan died. When David later became king, he inquired, "Is there yet anyone left of the house of Saul, that I may show him kindness for Jonathan's sake?" (2 Samuel 9:1). Jonathan's crippled son, Mephibosheth, was found and brought into the king's presence. Mephibosheth figured David was going to kill him, but David reassured him. "Do not fear, for I will surely show kindness to you for the sake of your father Jonathan, and will restore to you all the land of your grandfather Saul; and you shall eat at my table regularly" (2 Samuel 9:7).

Dee Brestin, author of *The Friendships of Women,* says, "It is in the account of the keeping of David's promise that we see perhaps the clearest reflection of Christ....And God says to us, though we are crippled in both feet, 'Don't be afraid...for I will surely show you kindness for the sake of My Son Jesus, and you will always eat at My table.' That's the promise, the commitment."[1] May we always seek to exemplify Jesus through our friendships, showing loyalty and commitment over the years.

Forgive Each Other

Even the best of friends disappoint us once in a while. We're all human, and sometimes our frailty gets the best of us. That's why we must forgive each other. James 1:19 suggests, "...Let every one be quick to hear, slow to speak and slow to anger." That's great wisdom for friendships!

But what about those friends who constantly hurt and betray us? Do we need to keep on forgiving them?

Absolutely yes, we need to forgive them. Any hint of unforgiveness will create a seed of bitterness in our hearts that will lead us straight into Satan's stronghold. Luke 6:45 warns us not to store evil in our hearts or it will spill out of our mouths.

But such a friendship needs to be evaluated. If someone constantly hurts you, I daresay she isn't a friend, and you probably should distance yourself from that relationship. If after reading these twenty-six characteristics of friendship, you're having a hard time finding very many that ring true with that person, ask God to guide you to other, truer friends.

Get Together with Each Other Often

After I started having children, I found it increasingly difficult to make time for my friends. I wanted to spend time with them and knew I needed their companionship, but other things seemed more pressing. Finally, I realized I needed to schedule time to be with them. Now, my husband and I give each other one night a week to be with our friends. On my night, he keeps the kids and vice versa. I would encourage you to try this. It has been great not only for my friendships but also for my marriage. After all, my husband can't meet all my relational needs, and I need time with godly girlfriends to get recharged. Then I have more to offer at home.

Hold Each Other Up

Exodus 17:8-13 tells a wonderful friendship story. Moses, Aaron, and Hur were on top of a hill watching Joshua fight the Amalekites. As long as Moses' hands held high the staff of the Lord, the Israelites were winning. But verse 11 says, "...whenever he lowered his hands, the Amalekites were winning" (NIV).

Have you ever grown weary doing all that's required of you? I know I have, especially in times of exacerbating circumstances. You know, when your husband has to be out of town on a business trip, or one of your loved ones is in the hospital, or you bring home a new baby, or (one of my personal favorites) when a snowstorm knocks your power out for more than a week. It's time to call in the reserves, those friends you know you can count on through thick and thin, just as Moses received a little help from his friends. The beautiful part of Moses' story is that it doesn't mention in the text that he asked for help. His friends recognized his need and stepped in to shoulder the burden. Verses 12 and 13 say, "When Moses' hands grew tired, they took a stone and put it under him and he sat on it. Aaron and Hur held his hands up—one on one side, one on the other—so that his hands remained steady till sunset. So Joshua overcame the Amalekite army with the sword" (NIV). What a great picture of victory, three friends side by side and arm-in-arm!

Inspire Each Other

What a treat to write this book with my partner in ministry, Sharon. But Sharon is much more than a partner; she is a close friend. In many ways she is my mentor. (Not because she's that much older but because she's journeyed a little farther down life's road.) Just by watching her live out all she encourages others to do, she's inspired me to be the kind of wife, mother, and homekeeper I need to be.

And the inspiration has worked vice versa. For years Sharon kept her amazing stories and other writings in a drawer, never thinking they would be read by anyone. When I read a few of her stories as possible material for *The Proverbs 31 Woman* newsletter, I encouraged her to pull them out of that drawer and send them to publishers. That next summer Sharon and I traveled together to the Christian Booksellers Convention, and since then Sharon has been busy creating books.

What a joy to inspire each other. Are you inspiring and being inspired by your friends?

Journey Through Life Together

Sometimes sweet friendships have bittersweet interruptions, times when circumstances are so overwhelming you can hardly keep your own head above water, much less muster the energy to maintain a friendship. This is the place where we find three women in the book of Ruth.

Ruth and Orpah are Naomi's daughters-in-law. All three women have been widowed, leaving a bitter Naomi without a husband or sons. The only family she has are her two daughters-in-law, but in Ruth 1:8-9 she sends them away. "Go back, each of you, to your mother's home. May the LORD show kindness to you, as you have shown to your dead and to me. May the LORD grant that each of you will find rest in the home of another husband" (NIV). At first both girls resisted, but after much persistence on Naomi's part, Orpah finally agreed to leave. But Ruth responded differently, choosing to stay with Naomi despite Naomi's protests.

Sometimes we must look past our hurt friend's reactions and remain steadfast. Fueled by the Holy Spirit's steadying power in us, we choose to press on during times of difficulty and continue life's journey together.

Know the Details of Each Other's Everyday Life

I've heard plenty of statistics about the number of words a woman speaks in any given day as opposed to the number a man will speak. Let's just say the women beat the men hands down. Just as a man is likely to speak fewer words, he can't take in as many words. I used to overload my husband with conversation only to have him respond with a glazed look. Why wasn't he interested in the intimate details of the mouse that gave birth to baby mice in my kitchen, my latest dieting attempt, and the vacation deal of the century the telemarketer called about today? Well, I finally figured out he wasn't indifferent, he just needs the Cliff Notes version.

My girlfriends, on the other hand, love to hear the details of my antics and can process every last word. And I want to hear the retelling of their day's events as well. The funny thing is that we know each other so well we can finish one another's sentences. I love knowing people who listen to the recounting of my everyday happenings, and my husband is thankful for those women as well.

Laugh with Each Other

For my birthday celebration with two friends, we decided to go to dinner and a movie. Well, this movie was supposed to be suspenseful, but about halfway through it turned scary. I was afraid when I watched *Bambi,* so it doesn't take much for me to shake in my seat. After nearly squeezing one of my friend's hands until it was purple and burying my face into the other's shoulder, we developed the giggles. We're talking the kind that causes the whole row of seats to shake. My fears were lost in the midst of laughing tears. I don't recall much about that movie, but I do know laughing with friends is one of the best remedies for whatever ails you.

Make Each Other Stronger

Have you ever noticed how many biblical characters come in pairs? Paul and Timothy, Mark and Barnabas, Elisha and Elijah, Elizabeth and Mary, and Ruth and Naomi, just to name a few. Why does God seem to pair up people to accomplish His great works? "Two are better than one because they have a good return for their labor. For if either of them falls, the one will lift up his companion. But woe to the one who falls when there is not another to lift him up...A cord of three stands is not quickly torn apart" (Ecclesiastes 4:9-12).

Now wait a second, I thought we were talking pairs. Where did three strands come from? The strongest bond a friendship can have is for two to be intertwined around the central strand of God!

Notice Each Other's Needs

What a blessing to have a friend anticipate your needs. I've had friends offer to watch my children or make me a meal, or one of them will send an encouraging note just when I'm feeling blue. Noticing your friend's needs will make her feel treasured. Don't put off doing something special for a friend who could use a little lift today.

A friend of mine has a great routine. On the 25th of every month, in honor of Jesus' birthday, she practices Kindness Day by doing something special for another person.

Open Up to Each Other

In *The Snow Queen,* a Hans Christian Andersen fairy tale, a "horrid mirror in which all good and great things were magnified and every flaw became very apparent"[2] exists. Yikes! I'm glad the mirrors in my home aren't like that.

But I'm also glad I don't have to carry the burden of my flaws by myself. I'm so thankful for my handful of godly friends whom I trust enough to share my uglies and ask them to pray for me and hold me accountable. We all have uglies, and no doubt we struggle with many of the same things, especially that one week of the month when we get what I call the "Princess Must Scream" syndrome…PMS. To have a friend we feel safe enough to open up to is a treasure and a necessity.

Women have a tendency to hide their secret sins under lock and key in their hearts. But that allows Satan to use these secrets against us. The beauty of opening up to a godly friend is that she will shine the light of God's truth on the uglies, which brings hope and healing. John 8:32 instructs that if we hold on to Jesus' teaching then we "shall know the truth, and the truth shall make [us] free."

Point Each Other to Christ

John 13:34-35 says, "A new commandment I give to you, that you love one another, even as I have loved you, that you also love one another. By this all men will know that you are My disciples, if you have love for one another." How did Jesus love us? Enough to give His life. While we may never be called on to make such a sacrifice, we will be called to love sacrificially. By loving each other this way, we will point people to Christ as well. To glorify God and to point people to Jesus is the highest honor and duty for friendships.

Quiet Each Other's Restless Heart

Have you ever walked into someone's home and envied what she possessed? Have you ever heard a husband say something to his wife that you've longed to hear from your spouse? We women are masters at having restless hearts. It takes a conscious effort to stop playing the comparison game.

Friends can help quiet each other's restless heart by reminding one another what they are thankful for rather than centering their conversations on what they feel they're lacking. Helping each other develop attitudes of gratitude brings happiness to the friendship and glory to God.

Respect Each Other's Differences

The division I see among women saddens me. If you're in a group of women and bring up the subject of working moms and stay-at-home moms, instantly hairs stand on end, battle lines are drawn, and tensions run high. Maybe that tension has affected some of your friendships. We should respect each other's differences and strive to help shoulder each other's burdens rather than condemning one another. The stay-at-home mom could make a meal for her friend who works. The working mom could offer to run an errand during her lunch hour for her friend who is at home with little ones. However friends choose to express their love for each other, they should look for ways to respect their differences.

Spur Each Other On to Godliness

When my friend Sheila and I met for lunch one day, she taught me a powerful lesson in spurring others on to godliness. The conversation turned to hearing God's voice and responding to it. Sheila told me of a time God told her to buy groceries for a family in need. At first she pushed aside the call to help this family. After all she was busy, and her family was going through a tough financial situation themselves. A few days later she called her friend to ask how things were going. Her friend told her they were fine except they had no food.

Instantly, Sheila's conscience was pricked. She admitted her disobedience to her friend, apologized, and made arrangements to meet so Sheila could deliver the food. While Sheila was loading the groceries, which totaled exactly $100, into her friend's car, a man walked up to Sheila's husband and said God told him to give this to them. He handed over a hundred-dollar bill.

Sheila taught me two lessons that day. One, we should all be more willing to listen to God's voice. Two, when God does amazing things, we must share them with our friends, thus multiplying the blessing and spurring them on to godliness.

Team Up with Each Other

Things are always more fun when you team up with a friend. I have a friend who is great at organizing but who struggles trying to decorate her home. I, on the other hand, love to decorate but struggle with organizing. So we teamed up and helped each other. She has taught me great tips on organizing and keeping things tidy, and I've helped her develop an eye for coordinating fabrics and using colors that make her and her family feel at home.

Team up with your friends. Find areas in which you can help them and they can assist you.

Understand Each Other

We would be wise to understand our friend's loveliness and "prickliness." Just as a beautiful rose has both fragrant, soft petals as well as sharp, hurtful thorns, so do our friends. Dee Brestin says, "After experiencing a few jabs into your soft tender flesh, you handle roses with more respect. A dedicated rose gardener, one who believes that the glory of the rose more than compensates for the occasional wounds it inflicts, learns to bear the pain and to handle roses in such a way that she is seldom jabbed."[3] In developing long-lasting friend-ships, we must learn to appreciate all that is wonderful about each other and all that isn't so wonderful. We would be wise to remember that what we consider flaws may simply be differences in opinion or personalities. Seek God to help you to understand your friends better.

Value Each Other

Recently, God pierced my heart with a question: Is this the greatest day of your life?

What an odd inquiry. *This is just an ordinary day,* I thought. I woke up, awakened the kids, fixed breakfast, woke up my husband, and went running. I returned from my run to tie bows around pigtails and ponytails, kiss every-one good-bye, and change the baby's diaper. I called a friend while I cleaned the kitchen and then called another while making the beds.

Then the question stirred my soul once more, only this time it came with a slight twist: If you had no children and then suddenly today you were blessed with them, wouldn't it be your greatest day ever? If you were paralyzed and then you suddenly could walk, wouldn't this be your greatest day ever? If you had no husband, then today God gave you a man who loved you and called you his wife, wouldn't this be your greatest day ever? If you had no home, then suddenly you were blessed with dishes to wash and beds to make, wouldn't it be the greatest day ever? If you had no friends, and then today you had two who were excited to have you phone them, wouldn't this be your greatest day ever?

Let's never forget how blessed we are and value our friendships—and everything else God has provided.

Withstand Trials Together

The room was packed with friends, down on their knees praying for a dear brother and sister in Christ. The couple had been accused falsely of a serious wrongdoing and needed the support, love, and most of all, the prayers of their friends. Though the trial was long, the couple weathered the storm. If you were to ask them how they made it through, they would tell you that, while they realized Christ pulled them through, their friends' steadfast love and prayers kept them afloat.

That reminds me of the campfire song I used to sing as a teenager. "They will know we are Christians by our love, by our love." The way we love each other in good times and bad speaks to the watching world. May the attractiveness of our friendships draw many to our Savior.

XYZ...eXamine Your Zest

I love the word "zest," which means "to add spice to." That's exactly what our friendships do. They enhance our lives and bring out a unique flavor. They also help preserve us and the godly heritage we're committed to. They add zip and zing during times of rejoicing, and they cry salty tears during times of sorrow. Just as a good pot of stew becomes great when the right spices are added, so are our lives made better with friends.

THIRTY-TWO

What a Friend!

Sharon

*A*s I read over Lysa's "ABCs of Friendship," my mind drifted to thoughts of my best friend, Jesus. Don't you love to receive letters from someone dear to you? My best Friend has written me many letters, but my favorite is John 13–17. Amazingly, all the aspects of friendship can be found there.

In this letter, Jesus tells me that He *accepts* me and has chosen me to be His friend (13:18a). He *believes* in me, and I believe in Him (16:27). Sometimes we *cry* together because He has experienced the same struggles I have and knows how I feel (15:18). He *defends* me by praying for my protection from the Evil One (17:11,15). He *exemplifies* how I am to relate to other people by being a servant leader (13:1-5) and *forgives* me when I am weak (16:32). We *get together* often, and I go to Him (14:18-19). One day we will be next-door neighbors (14:23). He *holds* me up by giving me the Holy Spirit (14:18) and *inspires* me to be spiritually productive (15:7). We are *journeying* through life together, both united in God (14:20).

Because I am no longer just a servant but Christ's friend, He *knows* every detail of my life and lets me in on the details of His (15:15). We *laugh* together, and He makes my joy complete (15:12). He *makes* me stronger, *notices* my needs, and understands I need help (14:16). I can always *open* up to Him and ask Him anything (16:24), and He opens up to me, teaching and explaining things the Father has taught Him. Jesus *points* me to God (14:9) and *quiets* my restless heart with His peace (14:27). He *respects* our differences, knows I am weak (14:29), and at the same time *spurs* me on to godliness and encourages me to obey God (14:15).

We *team* up together (14:12); He *understands* me because He is my counselor (14:26) and *values* me greatly (15:9). He *withstands* trials with me (17:12) and challenges me to *examine my zest* by evaluating how well I obey (14:23).

As Christian women, we never have to read about mentors and friendships and end up feeling neglected and alone. Jesus Christ is the best Friend anyone could have, for "greater love has no one than this, that one lay down his life for his friends" (15:13). In Him, we have everything we could ever ask for, every minute of every day.

Splashes from John

SHARON

*T*he sixth principle states that the Proverbs 31 woman speaks with wisdom and faithful instruction as she mentors and develops godly friendships. What a treasure God has given us in friendship. What a responsibility He has given us in mentoring. The word "friend" even sounds soothing while the word "mentor" sounds mental. One makes us feel fuzzy, and the other makes us feel faint. However, Jesus relieves our fears of mentoring and shows us that developing godly friendship and mentoring go hand in hand.

Once again, as we sit by the sixth pool, John 6 turns our attention to the sixth principle. Jesus created quite a stir after He healed the lame man by the pool in John 5. Then He and His disciples stole away to the north shore of the Sea of Galilee for a little time by themselves.

However, soon a large crowd sought Him out to witness more such miracles. Five thousand men—not to mention women and children—appeared on the scene like water bursting through a broken dam.

Jesus turned to Philip and asked, "Where are we to buy bread, that these may eat?" (verse 5b).

Jesus wasn't at a loss as to what to do. As a mentor, He asked a question to involve His students in the solution. The Bible tells us it was to test Philip (verse 6).

Philip calculated two hundred denarii, eight months' wages, would be needed but admitted that "would not be enough bread for each one to have a bite!" (verse 7 NIV).

Then Andrew piped up, "There is a lad here who has five barley loaves and two fish, but what are these for so many people?" (verse 9).

Jesus brought order to the scene and told everyone to sit down on the grass. He said a blessing over the boy's small lunch and handed the food to the disciples, who acted as waiters, serving the crowd. The food kept multiplying and multiplying—not just until the edge was taken off, not just until everyone was satisfied, but until everyone was filled. Twelve baskets of leftovers remained for the disciples to take home. (Jesus shows us that even in plenty we are not to be wasteful.)

Jesus didn't need His twelve friends to help Him perform this miracle. However, as a mentor, He included them in ministry. What a friend!

But His example of friendship doesn't stop there. After their life lesson on how God can do much with little, the disciples hopped in a boat to cross the Sea of Galilee (which is more like a large pool cupped between the hills than a sea). For some reason, Jesus stayed behind.

During the night, the winds picked up, and the little boat was tossed violently by the waves. At some point, the disciples looked up and saw Jesus walking on the water toward them. This frightened them more than the turbulent sea.

Jesus said, "It is I; don't be afraid." As soon as Jesus stepped in the boat, they were on the other side of the sea, where they were headed before the storm came up.

One quality of a godly friend is helping others to reach their goals and to get to where they need to be. No, we can't walk on water, calm the storms in our friends' lives, or land their boat where they want to go. But we can point them to the Friend who sticks closer than a brother.

In your relationships, are you allowing your friends to participate in God's work with you? Are you helping them get where they want to go? Are you leading them to the One who can help them get there?

Extend Yourself to Meet Community Needs

THIRTY-THREE

Reaching Out

SHARON

*P*rinciple 7: The Proverbs 31 woman shares the love of Christ by extending her hands to help with the needs in the community.

Looking out my den window, I noticed two of my neighbors puttering slowly down the street. Ernestine, with her bald head snuggled in a woolen cap, held tightly to Patti's supporting arm. Patti's chestnut hair, just two inches long, shone like a victor's crown—the crown of a cancer survivor.

In May 1998, Patti felt a lump in her breast and feared the worst. A doctor's visit confirmed she had breast cancer. For three months she endured chemotherapy followed by seven weeks of radiation, five days a week. As God would have it, her final treatment fell on Thanksgiving Day. Yes, she had much to be thankful for—a full life, a loving husband, and Ernestine Nevils, who had moved into the neighborhood in 1996.

When Ernestine moved next door to Patti, they connected as if they had known each other all their lives. Patti said, "Even though Ernestine is too young to be my mother, only fifteen years my senior, I feel as if God has given me just that, the gift of another mother." During Patti's cancer treatment, Ernestine was right by her side, an extension of Jesus' hands and feet providing love, encouragement, and support. By

July of that year, Patti had lost all her hair, and Ernestine was the one person, besides Patti's husband, with whom she felt comfortable not wearing her wig.

One year after her final radiation treatment, Patti was given the opportunity to return the kindness to Ernestine. In November 1999, a trip to the doctor revealed that Ernestine had lymphoma, cancer of the lymph nodes. Now Patti was the nurturer. She took Ernestine to her first chemotherapy and explained what to expect. She told Ernestine what to eat, where to go to have a wig made, and how to deal with depression.

"I never had to tell Patti what I needed," Ernestine remembered, "because she already knew, sometimes when I didn't even know myself. She'd say, 'Ernestine, I think you need to take a little walk. It'll make you feel better.' Now, if someone else had told me that, I might have said, 'Leave me alone. You don't know how I feel.' But Patti did know how I felt. She'd traveled this road just a few months before. I know without a shadow of a doubt that God moved me here, right next door to Patti. He is good."

I asked them both, "What does it mean to you to have each other's love and support?"

With tears in their eyes, they agreed, "I just can't explain it." But the looks on their faces said it all.

As I watched the twosome that day, I whispered a prayer, thanking God for the privilege He gives us of being His hands and feet to minister in the community, His strong arm to hold up a sister during times of struggle, and His heart to express compassion to a hurting world.

We've made it to the seventh and final pool of the waterfall. What started as rain from heaven has filled the first pool and spilled over to the second, third, fourth, fifth, and sixth pools. Then the life-giving water flows out into the Pacific Ocean and to the world. The seventh principle states, "The Proverbs 31 woman shares the love of Christ by extending her hands to help with the needs in the community." Together, let's look at what that means.

THIRTY-FOUR

Ripples in the Pool

SHARON

*I*n Jesus' last words to His disciples, He gave them a charge. "But you will receive power when the Holy Spirit comes on you; and you will be my witnesses in Jerusalem, and in all Judea and Samaria, and to the ends of the earth" (Acts 1:8 NIV). It seems only fitting that *A Woman's Secret to a Balanced Life* ends with that same charge.

We started at the mountaintop, focusing on developing a personal and ongoing relationship with Jesus Christ, and now we focus on the vast sea of people who need the rejuvenating, refreshing, regenerating power of our Savior. Jesus encouraged His disciples to reach out to three areas: first, in their hometown of Jerusalem; second, in the surrounding regions of Judea and Samaria; and finally, to the entire world.

When you throw a pebble into a pond, concentric circles emanate from its point of entry. Jesus' penetrating power has the same rippling effect, as He calls us to reach out to those around us, then a little farther out, and then even farther still.

In Our Jerusalem

Reaching out to the community begins right in our neighborhoods. Where you live is no accident. The apostle Luke said, "From one man he made every nation of men, that they should inhabit the whole earth; and he determined the times set for them and the exact places where they should live" (Acts 17:26 NIV). God could have put you in any nation during any time. In accordance with His perfect plan, He chose for you to occupy this particular time in history and your particular place.

When we become Christians, we're called ambassadors, or representatives, of Jesus Christ. When we share His love, it's as though He is making His appeal to the world through us (2 Corinthians 5:20). Only God can change hearts, but our feet must do the walking, our lips must do the praying, and our hands must do the serving.

John 1:14 says, "And the Word became flesh, and dwelt among us, and we beheld His glory, glory as of the only begotten from the Father, full of grace and truth." I love how Eugene Peterson paraphrases this verse in his book *The Message*: "The Word became flesh and blood, and moved into the neighborhood." As soon as you moved into your particular neighborhood, Christ in you moved there too. Our honor and privilege is to be His official representatives where we live.

Love Your Neighbor

Mary Lance Sisk, author of *Love Your Neighbor as Yourself,* offers a simple acrostic as a guide to ministering to your neighbors. **N**ourish the heavenly vision of reaching out to your neighbors. **E**valuate your neighborhood to see who is living there, perhaps by creating a neighborhood directory. **I**ntercede for your neighbors and possibly walk with two other Christians and pray for each house as you go past. **G**ather others to pray with you. **H**ave compassion for your neighbors. **B**uild relationships. **O**pen your home to others and perhaps invite neighbors to study God's Word with you. **R**ejoice in the opportunity you have to share Jesus Christ with those around you.[1]

I followed Mary Lance Sisk's advice for my neighborhood. First I nourished the idea that God had me in this neighborhood for a reason. I evaluated and realized many Christians and non-Christians peppered my streets. Two other neighbors joined me in praying for our neighbors, and we decided to prepare a Christmas tea to bring the women together. Forty-five neighborhood women showed up, and at the close of the tea we extended an invitation for them to join us in a Bible study. I'll never forget one woman sheepishly asked, "I've never studied the Bible before. Is it all right if I come?" Of course, I couldn't say yes fast enough!

We also sent out a questionnaire to all the homes and compiled a directory. Along with names, addresses, and phone numbers, the questions included inquiries about hobbies, ages of children, special interests, and availability of babysitters, pet sitters, and grass cutters. All but one neighbor of the seventy-five completed the survey and requested a copy of the finished product. The directory took away the feeling we were living among strangers and introduced us to each other. It also served as a prayer tool as I prayed for each family.

In the following years, I watched relationships grow and mature. We've cried when children went away to college, prayed for each other during hard times, offered monetary gifts during financial crises, opened up our homes for shared meals, cared for each other's children, cooked dinners for those who were ill, and gathered for going-away parties.

The Nearby Mission Field

During the years when a mother of young children finds it difficult to volunteer in the community, what better mission field could she explore than the one right next door? My friend Judy Turner is a mother of eight young children. When her seventy-two-year-old German neighbor lost her husband, Judy prayed, "God, what can I do to reach out to Betty and share your love with her?" Immediately, Judy felt God's reply, "Ask her to take evening walks with you." Betty welcomed the company, and the twosome have rarely missed a day strolling around the neighborhood.

"The Lord has given me a burden to make sure Betty feels loved and cared for," Judy explained. "I call her regularly to make sure she's OK. Each morning I walk down to the curb, pick up her newspaper, and tuck it in her door. As I do, I whisper a prayer, 'Good morning, Lord. Here's the newspaper for Your child, Betty.' I also pray for her protection and for special surprises to come her way. The children enjoy picking out goodies for Betty, such as fresh fruit, produce from our garden, or freshly baked bread. Small acts of kindness can be such a ray of light in an otherwise dreary day, especially when they have the face of a smiling child behind them."

After several months of walking with her neighbor, Judy asked, "Betty, do you know for sure where you are going when you die?"

"Not really," came Betty's reply. "I've tried to be a good person all my life, but I'm not sure if I've been good enough to go to heaven."

"Betty, that's not what the Bible says. Jesus wouldn't have come to die on the cross if we could be good enough to get to heaven."

"I never thought of it that way," Betty replied.

Judy went on to explain the abundance of God's grace and the assurance of salvation that's available to all who believe in Jesus Christ. On a quiet street, one late summer evening, Betty repeated the sinner's prayer and committed her life to Christ.

I'm sure when Judy and Betty are reunited in the heavenlies, they will enjoy many walks on the streets of gold. I do hope God puts their mansions side by side.

In Our Judea and Samaria

When Steven went off to middle school, I felt the Lord calling me to increase my sphere of ministry outside my neighborhood. So I spent some extended time at the first pool, praying for God's direction. One of my passions is the pro-life cause. The sanctity of life became more real to me after experiencing several years of infertility and the loss of a child through miscarriage.

So when I felt God calling me to volunteer as a counselor at a crisis pregnancy center, I questioned Him. "God, how can I volunteer at a place where most women don't want their children when my greatest desire is to have a houseful?"

I tried my best to talk God out of His prompting, but He wouldn't change His mind. He had a plan, so I did the only thing I could do: I obeyed.

I still remember sitting through those training classes, seeing the models of the developing fetus at different stages and thinking of my own child. I believe the instructors were questioning God as they watched me cry through each session. However difficult those days were, the words God spoke to Paul kept echoing in my head, "My grace is sufficient for you, for power is perfected in weakness" (2 Corinthians 12:9a).

Over the next two years, as a volunteer counselor, I learned more about what God can do with a heart dependent on Him. Moses became one of my heroes. Oh, how I identified with his arguments at the burning bush. "God, I can't do this. You've got the wrong guy. Pick someone else, for goodness' sake."

But each time Moses offered up an argument, God answered, "I will do it for you. I will do it for you. I will do it for you." And He did.

And God did it for me too. If He calls you to minister in your community, He will do it for you as well.

An ocean of needs exists in the world today, an ocean so vast one easily can feel overwhelmed and inadequate. When those emotions rise to the surface, I remember this story.

In Maine they tell of an old man walking home along the beach with his grandson. The beach was littered with starfish. The boy picked up a starfish they passed and threw it back into the sea. "If I left them here," the boy said, "they would dry up and die. I'm saving their lives."

Said the old man, "But the beach goes on for miles, and there are millions of starfish. What you are doing won't make any difference."

The boy looked at the starfish in his hand, gently threw it into the ocean, and answered, "It makes a difference to this one."

While this story encourages us to give freely of what we can, I would like to add one word of caution: I've watched many merciful women see the pool of community service and dive in headfirst, leaving their families to fend for themselves. We always must remember our relational priorities of God, husband, and children before reaching out to the community. A helpful maxim is "The need is not the call."

To the Ends of the Earth

As it turned out, being a volunteer counselor at the Charlotte Crisis Pregnancy Center was prep school for me. God was training me to depend on Him and had another plan that took my scope of ministry out further still. The pebble had landed in the waters of my life, and the circles were continuing to broaden.

In May 1995, I sensed an undeniable yet indefinable tug on my heart. I withdrew from many of my activities and decided to have an intermission of commitments on the stage of my life.

Again I identified with my friend Moses. I tended my "sheep" and kept an eye out for a burning bush to give me direction. During this intermission, I painted a mural, read God's Word, and wrote stories about how God was speaking to me in daily life. And while I was writing, I had the distinct impression that God still was writing the "introduction" of my life story. I was ready for a new chapter to begin.

One day, I explained this sense of being in limbo to a friend. "I have all these stories I've written, and I don't know what to do with them. Please pray that God will tell me what's next. I don't want to go forward until I hear from Him. I do know this, I love to write, but I never want to speak or say anything in front of people!"

Then Lysa TerKeurst of Proverbs 31 Ministries called and asked me to be a guest on Proverbs 31 Ministries radio program. She asked me to record five segments with her on how to be a supportive friend to someone who is experiencing infertility and five segments on inspirational stories I had written. With shaking knees, I reluctantly agreed. At the same time I reminded the Lord that this was the very thing I told Him I didn't want to do—speak.

After the recording session, Lysa said, "Sharon, I've been praying for a year that God would send me a partner, and today He's telling me that He has sent you. I want you to pray about becoming my partner in ministry."

Amazingly, we had been praying for the same number of months. God took two people who had a need and brought them together to meet the needs of women around the globe. Why didn't He answer our prayers the first month we prayed? I believe He was preparing us, molding us, and maturing us.

Now, I have to tell you, I argued with the Lord left and right. "God, You've got to be kidding. My voice is too Southern to do radio!" Then I thought about Billy Graham and Charles Stanley. (I hadn't met Beth Moore yet, God bless her.) "Well, Lord, my college degree is in dental hygiene, not public speaking!" Then I remembered His words to Moses, "I, even I, will be with your mouth, and teach you what you are to say" (Exodus 4:12b). "But God, I don't know anything about radio!" Then He reminded me of Bezalel and Oholiab whom He put in charge of working with gold and silver for the tabernacle. These guys had been making bricks with mud and straw as slaves for the Egyptians their entire lives, but God filled them with wisdom, understanding, and knowledge to do the task He called them to do.

So I agreed...to at least pray about it.

That summer my husband and I went to Bermuda for a romantic vacation. On one particular evening, Steve and I went dining at a five-star restaurant filled with men and women dressed in fine evening apparel. In one corner of the dining area, a four-man orchestra filled the room with fluid sounds of music from the '40s and '50s.

Steve said, "Come on, Sharon, let's take a spin on the dance floor."

"No way," I replied. "Nobody else is out there. I'm not going to be the only one out there with everyone staring at me. Suppose we mess up? I'd be embarrassed. Besides, it's been a long time since we've danced, and I don't remember all the steps. Let's wait until some other people dance; then I'll go."

Finally the first couple approached the floor. They looked like professional dancers, moving as one and never missing a beat. That didn't encourage me but only strengthened my resolve that the dance floor was no place for my feet to trod. Then a second couple, whose steps weren't quite as perfect, joined the first. Reluctantly, I agreed to go to a more secluded spot on the floor.

After a few minutes, I noticed a fourth couple approach the floor. The man was in a wheelchair. He was slightly balding with a neatly trimmed beard. On his left hand he wore a white glove, I guessed to cover a skin disease.

As the band played a peppy beat, the wife held her love's healthy right hand and danced with him. He spun her around as she stooped to conform to her husband's seated position. Lovingly, like a little fairy child, she danced around his chair, and when the orchestra slowed to a lazy, romantic melody, she pulled up a chair beside her beloved, and they held each other in a dancer's embrace.

My heart was so moved by this love story unfolding before my eyes that I had to turn my head and bury my face on Steve's shoulder so no one would see the tears streaming down my cheeks. As I did, I saw that every person in this rigid, formal dining room had tears trickling down their cheeks.

After watching this display of love and courage, I realized that my inhibitions of not wanting others to watch me because my steps weren't perfect were gone. And the Lord spoke to my heart. "Sharon, I want you to notice who moved this crowd to tears. Was it couple number one, with their perfect steps? Or was it the last couple who not only didn't have perfect steps but also had no steps at all? My child, it was the display of love, not perfection, that had an effect on the people watching."

The Lord doesn't expect our steps to be perfect. He just expects us to be obedient, to take the first step, and to let Him do the rest. The man in the wheelchair never even moved his feet; his wife did the moves for him. And I need to remember that the Lord will do it for me. I also need to remember that perfect steps aren't what the world so desperately longs for. The world isn't impressed by supposedly perfect people who live in perfect houses with perfect children. People are impressed by love—genuine, God-inspired love.

When we returned home, we attended a worship service in a church we didn't usually attend. A visiting preacher was to give the sermon. As he stepped to the podium, he said, "I'm not going to preach on the text that's listed in your bulletin, so just put it away. God has just laid another message on my heart."

He then proceeded to teach from John 2, in which Jesus turned the water to wine at the wedding feast of Cana. When the pastor read the verse, "His mother said to the servants, 'Whatever He says to you, do it,'" I turned to Steve. "Did you hear that?"

"Yes," he said. "I heard that. Why?"

"Why? Well, because that's God's answer to my prayer. 'Whatever He says to you, do it.'"

Well, that's how an insecure gal like me, who told the Lord she never wanted to say anything in front of people, began to speak all across the country about how to have unshakable confidence in Jesus Christ. That's how a woman who as a teenager read few books but owned every Cliff Notes known to humanity, became an author of several books. That's how a homemaker became involved in an international ministry.

In case I haven't made myself perfectly clear, let me underline this fact: This story isn't about me; it's about God. Since at one point He spoke through a donkey, I shouldn't be flattered.

As a matter of fact, most of the men and women He chose for ministry were weaklings, just like me, and perhaps like you. Gideon was hiding in a wine press when God called him to lead the Israelites into battle (Judges 6:11). Three of the four women Matthew mentioned in Jesus' lineage had sordid backgrounds. His disciples were mostly a band of uneducated fishermen.

A few years ago, on a visit to southern India, Anne Graham Lotz was taken to a soccer stadium full of thousands of expectant people and was asked to give an evangelistic message like her daddy. Although Anne told her hosts evangelistic messages weren't her forte, she stepped into the pulpit and preached. She said, "I was sitting there thinking, 'I'm an American housewife. I don't belong here.' But I stepped aside and let God take over. And it's amazing what He can do."[2]

How do you know if God is calling you to increase your scope of ministry? No formula or ten-step outline makes the message clear. You know by developing a deep relationship with the Lord, by spending hours by the first pool, and by learning to listen to His voice. Then, when you hear His call, you jump in with both feet but never let go of His hand.

Areas of Service

God can call us to do anything He wants, regardless of apparent spiritual gifts or personality types. However, I have noticed a certain pattern among those in ministry. God uses our past experiences as a springboard. He turns the miseries of the past into ministries of the present.

Anna Lisa was divorced by her husband and left destitute. Thirty years later, God blessed her financially, and she now has established a day care for single mothers as well as a law office to support disenfranchised women. Chris was devastated after finding out that her teenage daughter had an abortion. She now serves as an administrator of a crisis pregnancy center. Margaret was a breast cancer survivor and opened a boutique specializing in clothes for those who have had mastectomies. Joni Eareckson Tada became a paraplegic after a diving accident and now has a ministry for handicapped people all around the globe. Do you see a pattern here?

I believe past tragedies are like treasures God has given us. Oh, they may not seem like treasures at the time, but their value becomes apparent when we decide to use those experiences for good.

In Matthew 25, Jesus told a parable about a wealthy landowner who was preparing to go on a trip. After carefully considering the abilities of three of his servants, he entrusted them with talents, or silver coins. Two servants invested and doubled their treasure. The third servant buried the master's talent in the sand. When the master returned, he applauded each of the faithful servants with the words, "Well done, good and faithful servant! You have been faithful with a few things, I will put you in charge of many things" (verse 21 NIV). But he was terribly disappointed in and angry with the servant who buried his talent in the sand, and he threw the fellow off the land.

I believe our past struggles are like those talents, and the Master is pleased when we invest them in others. Likewise, I believe He isn't pleased when we hide our struggles because of fear, embarrassment, or pride and don't invest in His children.

Take a few minutes to think about your life. What have you gone through that God could possibly be asking you to invest in others? Has He freed you from the shame of a scandalous past? Has He brought you through an abusive marriage? Has He delivered you from emotional turmoil? Has He bound up the wounds of past child abuse? Remember, God comforts us, not to make us comfortable, but to make us comfortable. Will you go wherever He calls?

THIRTY-FIVE

Butterflies, Brides, and the Bountiful Harvest

LYSA

*W*hen God asked me if I would go wherever He called, I flippantly said, "Sure, God. I'll go tell women how to love their husbands and children. I'll go encourage the saints and win the sinners over to you by telling them the good parts of my Christian walk. Now, God, You do understand I'll never share a few minor details about my life, right?"

God seemed silent. Again, I felt Him speaking to my heart, "Will you go?"

Tears welled up in my eyes, and my throat tightened. "What do You want from me, God? You're a loving God; why would You call me to tell people about things that have brought such anguish to my life? That certainly can't bring glory to You or draw others into a closer walk with You. No, I'll never share my life story."

Thoughts of people's rejecting stares and whispers seared my heart. If I told people about my past, I would end up in a modern-day version of *The Scarlet Letter*. I could almost read the headlines, "Woman in Christian ministry...her story will shock you."

At that point in my Christian life, I was like a caterpillar inside a cocoon. I had crawled in as a pretty content little caterpillar. Soon I wasn't a caterpillar but not quite a butterfly either. Struggling and fighting to grow and change, I wondered why a good God would put me through such an experience. Then God whispered through the cocoon's walls, "When you come out of there, will you tell people about the great things I have done?"

"What?" I answered, a bit dazed. "Is that thought supposed to comfort me?" I was on a search for healing, not humiliation. I wanted God to use the good about me, not the ugly.

But as I grew and changed, my struggle within the cocoon began to make sense. I had to work to gain the strength to fly. No struggle, no flight.

Once freed from the cocoon, I flitted and fluttered about. Then something caught my eye in the pond below. I darted left to take a closer look. It followed. I darted up and down and right and back, then left again. My reflection followed my every move. I had thought I was a caterpillar with wings attached. But then I saw I was a brand-new creature, made in the image of something more beautiful than I ever could have imagined.

I had no time to waste. I hurried off to tell other caterpillars my story...my whole story. Since then I've ended up in some pretty amazing places...

Kathryn's Story

My husband owns a Chick-fil-A franchise, a quick-service restaurant that offers delicious chicken. Because of the nature of our business, we employ many teenagers, including at one time, a girl named Kathryn. Her great attitude and solid work ethic made her a star employee. Then Kathryn's demeanor changed. Her perky smile had turned to a decided frown; her bright spirits were dampened. Kathryn was pregnant and was faced with a decision no young girl should have to handle. Because of her family's religious background and cultural tradition, the only logical choice, she reasoned at the time, was to have an abortion. The appointment was set.

One of our managers became concerned about Kathryn's changed attitude. Then came the request for a few days off for emergency surgery, and the manager suspected Kathryn might be pregnant. So the manager called me. She knew my story might help Kathryn and asked me to step in.

I phoned Kathryn and invited her to join me for lunch that very day. At the start of our conversation, I told Kathryn I wanted to share a part of my life story with her. Just a few minutes into my story, Kathryn's eyes filled with tears, and I knew our suspicions were confirmed.

I explained to Kathryn that she wasn't alone and that we could find people to help her. She agreed to postpone the abortion until after we could go to our local crisis pregnancy center for an ultrasound. After the ultrasound, abortion was never mentioned again.

About a year later, Kathryn, who had since moved out of town, called and asked if we could meet for lunch. I'll never forget watching her hold her beautiful son. He giggled and smiled and grabbed at her shirt. His tiny fingers held on to her as if to say, "I love my mommy. She makes me feel safe and happy." Kathryn reached across the table and held my hand. "How can I ever thank you?" I just smiled and replied, "Your son just did."

Daniela's Story

Daniela and I met at a small Bible study I was teaching. A friend of mine had taken this group of women from all sorts of religious backgrounds through a time of spiritual discussions and felt they were now ready to deepen their spiritual journey. I was reluctant at first to take on such a challenge. What if they thought I was some kind of Christian fruit loop? What if they asked me questions I didn't know how to answer? Did I really have the time to invest in this type of commitment?

I almost said no. But after praying, I decided to accept the invitation.

I'm so glad I did. I grew to love all the women in that group but developed a special bond with Daniela. After a few meetings, Daniela asked if we could get together outside of the Bible study to talk about some questions she had.

I agreed, and we met for a lengthy breakfast. She told me she had grown up Catholic and had a pretty negative view of Christians before meeting me. Then she said, "When I hear you talk and I look into your eyes, I see a Jesus in you that I want to get to know." Daniela wasn't attracted to me but to Jesus, who was pouring His love, mercy, and grace through the many cracks in my imperfect vessel into my new friend's life.

When we parted, I prayed long and hard for her to accept Jesus as her Savior. I prayed that Jesus would pursue her as never before and that she would discover and accept His truth.

A few weeks later, she called and asked if we could meet again. We talked for hours once more. After answering her questions, I asked her what was holding her back from accepting the Lord. She said she didn't want to live the rest of her life feeling guilty for not being able to live up to the standard of being a good Christian. After we made a quick trip to Romans 8:1 and John 8:32, God's Word assured her that Jesus came to set her free, not to condemn her. Then, right there in my kitchen, Daniela was ushered from darkness into His amazing light. What a privilege to hold her hand and to watch God stamp "forgiven and set free" across the pages of her life.

A Pastor's Story

I received a call late one night from a youth pastor in Florida. He told me of a girl in his youth group who had just found out she was pregnant for the second time this year. Her first time had ended in an abortion. He feared she would repeat that decision because her parents were pressuring her. Would I be willing to talk with her and her parents?

I immediately agreed and told him to have her call me. As we were about to hang up, he said, "Oh, and one more thing; her dad is the senior pastor."

I had no idea what I would say to this hurting family. They knew the Scriptures. They knew the right answers. But fear and shame were dancing across the stage of their lives.

All I could think to do was to tell my story and how Jesus had set me free from fear and shame. During our time together, God started a miracle in the pastor's heart and in his family's life.

A few weeks later, I received a letter from the pastor's wife. She told me how she had grieved for the grandchild they had lost to her daughter's previous abortion. She also told me how her husband's heart had been transformed. He realized his fear of being judged and rejected by his congregation had caused pain to his family. To his wife's surprise, he admitted his mistake to his congregation and publicly acknowledged his daughter's pregnancy and his commitment to support her. After church that day, everyone in the congregation came forward to give his or her support and love to the pastor's family.

Again, this outcome had nothing to do with me or my abilities. I'm not a counselor, but I was willing to be used by the Mighty Counselor. In each of these stories, God called me to take the hand of one of His precious children and to walk to the edge of the river where His living water flows.

As I testified of His healing power, these hurting souls felt safe to test the waters for themselves. What they found was a love so amazing that it had the ability to drown out Satan's cruel lies. Watching these redeemed people splash about in God's goodness and grace has helped me to heal from my mistakes as I see Him use for His glory the very things I thought made me unusable. Three little stories with God-sized results.

I must say that each time God calls me to do something, I don't always answer Him as a mighty and brave warrior with my spiritual armor intact and my sword of the Spirit flashing. Many times feelings of inadequacy, fear, and sometimes laziness keep me from charging ahead.

Tim Hansel, author of *Holy Sweat,* writes, "Our hearts beat excitedly over stories of people like Abraham and Moses, yet we fail to recognize that they were as frail and nervous as we are. We stand in awe of Moses at the burning bush: 'Now there is a bush that burns,' we say. 'I would like to be a bush like that, but I'm just a heap of ashes.' And that's as far as we get. We discuss the phenomenon of what God can do in a life, tell amazing stories about it, praise it—but then resign ourselves to being nothing more than what we think we are, a mere bystander, resigned to sitting in the balcony among spectators. But it is not the bush that sustains the flame. It is God in the bush, and so, any old bush will do!"[1]

How absurd to think that, after God calls me, He wouldn't complete the call by manifesting His power in my weakness. He calls. He equips. Lives are changed. He is glorified.

Edmund Burke, an eighteenth century Irish statesman, once said, "The only thing necessary for the triumph of evil is for good men to do nothing." I know I am only one, but I'm committed to do whatever God calls me to do, go wherever God calls me to go, and give whatever God calls me to give. God needs nothing more than one willing heart to change the world.

A few Sundays ago my pastor asked if someone would give him a twenty-dollar bill. He told us that whoever did so wouldn't get his twenty dollars back. No one came forward. He asked again, and again no one came. Then, he asked if anyone would give him one dollar. Finally, a man from the back came forward and handed over a dollar.

As the man turned to leave, my pastor stopped him. "I told you you wouldn't get your dollar back, and you won't. You'll get ten in its place." I can't help but wonder what the pastor might have given had someone handed him a twenty.

That's so like our God. "Give, and it will be given to you; good measure, pressed down, shaken together, running over, they will pour into your lap. For by your standard of measure it will be measured to you in return" (Luke 6:38).

How I wish we could all see life with eyes fixed on eternity. If our perspective hovered in the heavenlies rather than on Earth, we wouldn't expend so much energy on the toils and troubles of this life but would work more for the kingdom's sake. And we constantly would dream about home. Our real home. The home where our souls long to be.

Once we reach the Great Beyond, we'll be reunited with our Bridegroom. He'll whisper to us, "Well done, my beautiful bride." And we'll respond, "Thank You. Thank You for the struggles and heartaches it took to prepare me for this moment. Thank You for allowing me to be Your servant, Your friend, Your bride. Thank You for teaching me, molding me, and using me for Your glory."

My sweet sister, ready yourself for your Beloved. Don't serve out of obligation or duty. Serve out of your heart's overflow of His love.

Jesus said, "Open your eyes and look at the fields! They are ripe for harvest" (John 4:35b NIV). Spread your wings, butterfly, and fly!

Splashes from John

SHARON

*S*tanding now at the foot of the mountain, the one-mile expanse of the seven waterfalls appears as a fluid, carpeted staircase. Everything about the scene shouts of life: the sound of rushing waters, the growth of ferns on slippery rocks, the display of African tulip trees bursting with orange-red blossoms, the rattling of bamboo moving in the breeze, the clamor of tourists climbing up and down the hillside, the giggling of children splashing in the pools.

I can't bring myself to sit by the seventh pool. As it spills out into the Pacific Ocean, something or someone calls me to stand and prepare to move forward.

The seventh principle states that the Proverbs 31 woman shares the love of Christ by extending her hands to help with the needs in the community.

In John 7, Jesus tells us how to move forward and begin to flow into the ocean of need. This chapter takes place during a celebration time called the Feast of Booths.

Jesus' brothers didn't seem to take kindly to all the attention He was receiving. They taunted and nagged him to go to the festivities and publicly proclaim that He was the Son of God. They said something like, "Hey, Big Guy, why don't you stop doing these miracles when not many people are around? Go public! You'll be famous! Why wait? Go with us to Jerusalem."

In response to their prodding, Jesus gives us an example of waiting on the Lord. He didn't allow His brothers to move Him before God said the time was right. So Jesus didn't go into Jerusalem with His brothers but waited until they were out of sight. Then, on the last day of festivities, God gave the go-ahead, and Jesus slipped into the temple when no one was looking.

He went public with His message, regardless of the consequences that were sure to come. The people listened and marveled. "How has this man become learned, having never been educated?" (verse 15).

I have no doubt that, as I've spoken to hundreds of women across the country, many have asked the same question. I'm sure my high school English teacher marvels that a girl who couldn't be bothered with reading a book could write books. I'm convinced that friends who know of my heavy sack of insecurities are amazed that I teach women how to have unshakable confidence in Christ. Likewise, Lysa's marriage counselors from her early years probably shake their heads in bewilderment when they think of her leading marriage improvement seminars. The answer to these mysteries is simple: God's transforming power.

Jesus admitted that the message He preached wasn't His own, but "His who sent Me" (verse 16).

On the last day of the Feast of Booths, the priests paraded from the temple to the pool of Siloam. There they drew water from the pool and poured it on the altar while reciting Isaiah 12:3, "With joy you will draw water from the wells of salvation" (NIV). They did this in memory of God's providing water to the Israelites in the desert.[1]

On this last day of the Feast of Booths, Jesus stood and proclaimed what the true water of salvation was. The water the priests commemorated was temporary. The water Jesus proclaimed was permanent. He said, "If any man is thirsty, let him come to Me and drink. He who believes in Me, as the Scripture said, 'From his innermost being shall flow rivers of living water'" (verses 37b-38).

Jesus was speaking of the Holy Spirit, who was to be given to all believers at Pentecost. It is because of those rivers of living water that an insecure little girl can become a bold witness for Christ and minister in the community. It is because of the rivers of living water that an abused little girl can share the hope of the Savior with the world. It is because of the rivers of living water that two little girls who had less than ideal home lives can work with a ministry that has as its logo "Touching women's hearts, building godly homes." Rivers of living water flowing in us, flowing through us, and spilling out from us.

In Acts 1:8, Jesus said, "But you shall receive power when the Holy Spirit has come upon you; and you shall be My witnesses both in Jerusalem, and in all Judea and Samaria, and even to the remotest part of the earth." Shortly after this announcement, the Holy Spirit fell on the disciples, and the men who had deserted Jesus out of fear a few days before began boldly to preach the Gospel, even if it meant death.

The Holy Spirit has come and now lives in each believer. As we turn to face the ocean of opportunities, will we share Christ's love with a hurting world? Your world may be your neighborhood, your city, or on foreign shores. Whatever the case, it is Jesus' love flowing through you that will change the world.

THIRTY-SIX

See You at the Top

LYSA

I can't tell you the number of times Sharon and I have been asked how we find the time, energy, and motivation to fulfill our roles with Proverbs 31 Ministries. I guess it's the same impetus that gives people the desire to climb a mountain. Once you've seen the view from the top, you want not only to reach the summit again, but you also want to take others with you.

We've seen the top. We've seen women give their hearts to Christ. We've seen wives fall back in love with their husbands, and we've seen marriage commitments renewed. We've wiped the tears of discouraged mothers and helped them to set their feet back on the right path. Jesus' love working through this ministry is what keeps us climbing.

Keep on Going

A climber's heart to overcome all obstacles was shown on a newsmagazine show, *Turning Point,* I saw one night. The episode was entitled "Everest: Mountain Without Mercy."[1] Diane Sawyer interviewed several survivors of the May 1996 tragedy in which eleven men and women died trying to reach Mt. Everest's summit.

One interview in particular caught my attention, that of Dr. Seaborn "Beck" Weathers. Weathers didn't make the ascent to the top of Everest. His eyesight gave out at 27,500 feet. At that altitude, a person must wear an oxygen mask to have enough air to survive. People become disoriented easily and experience various ailments including blurred vision.

Weathers' instructor told him it would be too dangerous to continue and that Weathers should wait for the instructor to pick him up on the descent. His instructor never returned.

A terrible storm with hurricane-like winds descended on the climbers. Another instructor, who was helping a group of struggling climbers, came across Weathers and helped him down to 26,000 feet. By then everyone's oxygen tank was empty, and most were too weak to continue. The instructor left the group to search for help.

By the time help returned, Weathers lay unconscious, barely breathing, with parts of his flesh exposed and frozen. The rescuers, weak themselves, determined to save others who seemed to have a better chance of survival and left Dr. Beck Weathers for dead. He was only 300 yards from camp.

Several hours later something clicked on in Weathers' hypothermic, comatose brain that compelled him to get up and find the camp. He later told Sawyers, "The point that I woke up, my motivation was pretty clear. I could sit there and see my family in front of me, and I wasn't going to give up."

Still partially blind and without oxygen, Weathers pulled off his pack, chipped some of the ice off his face, and stumbled toward where he believed the camp might be, based on the wind's direction. If he had gone the opposite way, he would have stumbled off a cliff to certain death.

Weathers said, "All I knew was that as long as my legs would run and I could stand up, I was going to move toward that camp, and if I fell down, I was going to get up. And if I fell down again, I was going to get up. And I was going to keep moving till I either hit that camp, I couldn't get up at all, or I walked off the face of that mountain."

Spiritual Mountain Climbing

Tears welled up in my eyes as I watched this man with half his face missing, his right hand amputated, and the fingers from his left hand gone. If this man was passionate enough about mountain climbing to risk life and limb, how much more should I be passionate and willing to risk it all to live out each of the seven principles we've explored together.

Dr. Beck Weathers later said in a *National Geographic* article, "When a middle-aged guy like me can survive that, it gives truth to the possibility that this kind of strength resides in each of us."[2]

So here we stand, not at the summit of a mountain but beside the seventh pool. We've cascaded our way through the other pools, spending time wading and splashing in each. Maybe you glided with ease through some and trudged with great effort through others. Nonetheless, you made it through.

But we can't stand here at the bottom for long. We must now ascend back to the top. What propels us to continually climb? I pray your motivation is the same as Sharon's and mine: You've seen the view from the top, and you can't wait to return, taking others with you.

Press on! There will be storms. There will be hard times. There will be times when you want to lie down and quit. But take heart and keep going. Philippians 4:13 says, "I can do all things through [Christ] who strengthens me." He strengthens you to do both the things you want to do and those you don't. To borrow a thought from Dr. Beck Weathers, "If you fall down, get up. And if you fall down again, get up."

See you at the top!

A
Bible
Study

Introduction

Now that you've read *A Woman's Secret to a Balanced Life*, we invite you to dive deeper into God's Word and learn more about refreshing ways to prioritize your life. We pray that you will be like a tree planted by streams of living water which produces fruit in due season (Psalm 1:3).

This study guide has two lessons for each of the seven principles. The studies will help you seek the Lord for ways to keep your priorities in order and be all that He has created you to be. You might want to gather together a group of other women or use this guide as a personal devotion. In any case, we know you will be blessed by spending time in His Word.

Personal Relationship

*I*sn't it amazing that the God of the universe desires to have a personal relationship with you? As a matter of fact, the first question asked in the Bible expresses His desire to fellowship with His people (Genesis 3:9).

Look up the following verses and note the words God uses to help us understand His relationship with us.

1. What did God call Moses? (Exodus 33:11)

2. How did Jesus refer to His disciples? (John 15:15)

3. The Song of Solomon is a metaphor of Christ's relationship with the church. In this book, which "character" is Christ? (Song of Solomon 5:10)

4. What does that say about His relationship to us?

5. In Psalm 23, God is referred to as our _____, and we are His_____.

6. In John 10:1-6, Jesus is referred to as our _____, and we are His _____.

7. In Matthew 7:7-11, God is referred to as our _____, and we are His _____.

8. In John 15:1-8, Jesus is referred to as the _____, and we are the _____.

9. In Isaiah 64:8, God is referred to as the _____, and we are the _____.

10. In Matthew 25:1,6 and Revelation 18:23, Jesus is referred to as the _____, and we are the _____.

11. What do all these analogies have in common? What does that tell you about our relationship with God?

12. Nothing could be more intimate than the relationship of a bride to her bridegroom. Let's look at what the Bible has to say about our role as the bride of Christ. How does God feel about you? (Isaiah 62:5)

13. How did John the Baptist refer to Jesus in John 3:29?

14. In ancient times, the bridegroom came in the middle of the night to get his bride. She always had to be ready because she didn't know the hour or the day he would come. What is the message of Matthew 25:1-13 to you?

15. What are some ways we can make ourselves ready for our Bridegroom?

16. Read Jeremiah 2:2. Sometimes the bridegroom may take the bride to places she doesn't necessarily want to go. But what is a young bride in love usually willing to do?

17. Sometimes those places may seem like barren desert. What is Jesus, our Bridegroom, able to do in a desert place? (Isaiah 41:18)

18. What desert places are in your life? How can you let the Bridegroom transform them?

19. The Bible is a wonderful love letter from God to you. It is very personal. If you knew you were going to be leaving your loved ones and could write one last letter, what would you say? How would your loved ones feel about that letter? At some point, when you have a good block of quiet time, go back and read John 14–17. These were Jesus' last words to His disciples before the crucifixion, and they also are meant for you.

Personal Relationship

*I*n the last lesson, we looked at how God desires a personal relationship with us. We also focused on Jesus Christ as our Bridegroom. Now let's look at our relationship with God as the vine and us as the branches.

1. Read John 15:1-8.

2. What is the relationship between a vine and its branches?

3. What needs must be met for the branches to grow and bear fruit?

4. Jeremiah 17:5-10 draws a picture of two types of trees. In what ways are the trees alike? In what ways are they different?

5. Read Psalm 1:1-3 and describe what happens when a person delights in the Lord.

6. To be like a tree planted by streams of water, we need to sink our roots into God's Word. How does Jesus describe the water that He can give, in John 4:10?

7. What do you think the author of Hebrews meant when he described God's Word as "living" in verse 4:12?

8. What do these verses say about the Word?
   Psalm 119:105

   2 Timothy 3:16

9. What do the verses on God's Word mean to your life?

10. What is our instruction in Proverbs 4:23? What is a wellspring?

11. How did Jesus guard His heart when He was tempted by Satan in the desert? (Matthew 4:1-11)

12. What is the result of knowing God as Paul did? (Philippians 4:6-7)

13. What is a key ingredient to an effective prayer life? (1 John 5:14) How do you know God's will?

14. How does God's Word help us to fulfill the role of branches to God's vine?

LESSON 3

A Wife of Noble Character

1. Read Proverbs 31:10-31 and list the qualities that made this wife excellent.

2. What do we know about her husband from these verses?

3. What kinds of choices has she made that make her worthy of praise?

4. According to 2 Peter 1:3, whose power must we rely on to make good choices?

5. What kind of knowledge enables us to make those choices?

6. Who wants to keep us from making those choices? (Ephesians 6:12)

7. Besides God's power, what enables us to overcome those forces? (2 Peter 1:4-7)

8. How does the passage in 2 Peter translate into being an excellent wife?

9. Find a verse in God's Word that deals with a particular struggle in your marriage. You could use a concordance to help you locate the verse. Record it here and meditate on it often.

The Oneness God Intends

1. Read Genesis 2:24. The Hebrew word for "one" is *echad,* which means "alike, altogether, or all at once." Write down ways that you and your husband practice the oneness God intends for a husband and wife.

   Physically:

   Spiritually:

   Emotionally:

2. This same word, *echad,* is used in Deuteronomy 6:4. Read this verse. With whom is the Father one according to John 17:21 and John 16:13-15? In what ways do you think these three are one?

3. How does marriage reflect that same oneness? In what ways is it different?

4. How was the oneness of the husband and wife disrupted in Genesis 3:7?

5. How is shame still a threat to marital oneness?

6. What are some ways to protect a marriage from the threat of shame physically, spiritually, and emotionally?

7. What other threat to marital oneness is found in Genesis 3:12?

8. Blame leads to a dangerous cycle: blame, bitterness, brokenness. How did Adam and Eve exemplify each of these stages?

9. Note after each of the following verses how to combat shame and blaming.

   a. Ephesians 4:29

   b. Ephesians 5:33

   c. Colossians 3:12-14

   d. 1 Peter 3:9

10. Write out Ephesians 4:31-32 as a prayer for oneness in your marriage.

LESSON 5

Making the Most of Motherhood

1. What do you think Proverbs 3:3 (NIV) means when it says to bind love and faithfulness around your neck and write them on the tablet of your heart?

2. How does that especially apply to mothers?

3. What encouragement does Galatians 6:9 offer to weary mothers?

4. What rewards are offered to a mom in Proverbs 31:28-31?

5. According to Colossians 1:11, where does our strength and endurance come from? What prevents you from experiencing His endurance and patience?

6. What does Luke 6:45 reveal about the words we speak around our children? If we want to change our words, what must we change first?

7. Galatians 5:22-23 provides us with a gauge for our behavior. Fill out the following chart, listing the attribute that is the opposite of the Spirit-filled quality.

Response of the Flesh	Response of the Spirit
	Love
	Joy
	Peace
	Patience
	Kindness
	Goodness
	Faithfulness
	Gentleness
	Self-control

8. Ask God to reveal areas in your life that are adversely affecting you as a mother. Then write down how to transform those negative qualities with the sweet fruit of the Spirit.

9. Read Deuteronomy 6:6-8. List some practical ways you can share God's love with your children as you:

Sit at home

Walk along the road

Lie down

Get up

The Mommy Factor

1. What ideas for praying for your children do you find in Ephesians 3:16-17?

2. What guidance does Ephesians 3:18-19 provide you in what to teach your children?

3. According to Ephesians 3:20-21, what should your children understand about God?

4. What encouragement can mothers draw from Jeremiah 29:11 for their children?

5. What diversions threaten your relationship with your children?

6. How can you protect yourself and your children from each diversion?

7. Read Psalm 90:12. Number the days you have left with each of your children. Take 18 and subtract their present age. Multiply that number by 365.

8. How much time do you spend each week with your children doing what they want to do?

9. How many times a week does your family eat a meal together?

10. What changes could you make that would enable you to invest more quality time with your children?

11. What can you do this week with your kids?

LESSON 7

Hospitality

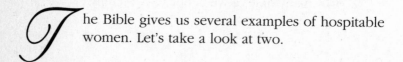he Bible gives us several examples of hospitable women. Let's take a look at two.

1. Read 2 Kings 4:8-10.

What did the Shunammite woman offer Elisha?

What was her financial status?

How would you describe what she offered? Extravagant? Simple? Comfortable?

Why did she make the offer?

What was Elisha's response to her?

The blessings she received from showing hospitality didn't end at verse 17. Read on through verse 37. What continued blessing did God bestow?

2. God used another woman to show hospitality to yet another prophet with a similar name. Read 1 Kings 17:7-24.

How are these two hospitable women different?

Was what this woman did for Elijah extravagant? Simple?

What was to be her blessing?

3. What conclusions can you draw by comparing these two examples of hospitality?

4. The ultimate guideline for hospitality is found in Matthew 7:12. What makes you feel loved and welcomed in someone's home?

5. We can also learn from negative experiences. Think of a time when you didn't feel comfortable in someone's home. What did they do or not do to foster that feeling?

6. Jesus was exemplary in offering hospitality. What do you learn from Him in the following verses?

Mark 10:45

Luke 22:27

John 13:1-17

John 21:9-14

7. What admonition does Peter give us in continuing Christ's example of hospitality in 1 Peter 4:9-11?

8. What does Peter say about our service and our speech in those verses?

9. What are some ways you can show hospitality in your home?

LESSON 8

Organization

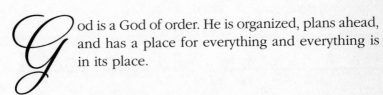

od is a God of order. He is organized, plans ahead, and has a place for everything and everything is in its place.

1. Read Genesis 1:1-7 and list the order in which Creation was made.

2. Suppose the order had been mixed up? (Such as the plants being created before light.) What would have been the outcome?

3. I'll not ask you to read all of Exodus 26–32, but flip through these pages of your Bible and scan the subheadings. Note God's specific plans for the tabernacle and list a few of them. What does this tell you about God's idea of order?

4. What do you learn about God from 1 Corinthians 14:33, 40?

5. How can being organized make your home run more smoothly?

6. How can order affect the ambiance of your home?

7. In which areas could your home be more orderly?

8. Read Philippians 4:13. What hope does it offer regarding putting life in order?

9. We all need help from time to time. Many of us need to learn the art of delegation.

   How did the disciples learn to delegate in Acts 6:1-6?

   How did Jethro, Moses' father-in-law, teach Moses to delegate in Exodus 18:14-24? What did Jethro see happening to Moses when he tried to do everything himself?

   In what areas of your life are you overtaxed? To whom could you delegate?

10. Write out Colossians 3:23 as a motto for homekeeping.

11. More important than an organized home is a pleasant and peaceful home. In what ways does attitude create a warm and loving environment, according to the following verses?

Proverbs 15:17

Proverbs 17:1

Proverbs 21:19

Proverbs 25:24

Proverbs 27:15

Proverbs 31:10

LESSON 9

Time Out!

1. Why do sports teams call for a time-out during a game?

2. Why, according to Matthew 7:21, is it important for us periodically to call time-out?

3. Read John 10:7-14. How is a shepherd like a coach?

4. In what ways could you let the shepherd dictate how your time in the game of life is to be spent?

5. Who is the thief in verse 10? How does he steal our time?

6. When Christ said He came to give us a full life, what do you think He meant it to be full of?

7. According to Matthew 6:33, what should be our first time-priority?

8. Read Ecclesiastes 3:1-8. In what ways do these verses console you regarding how you spend your time? In what ways do they challenge you?

9. Write down the activities from these verses you feel God is calling you to take a time-out to concentrate on.

10. Pull out your calendar and set aside time for those activities.

Being a Faithful Money Manager

1. According to Matthew 6:24-25, what criteria should you use to determine your view of money?

2. One classic sign that material desires have mastered someone is worry. According to the verses in Matthew, what should you do when you worry?

3. Read these verses and record what God says to you through each:

   Matthew 6:26

   Matthew 6:32

4. What does God provide for the birds? What will God provide for you?

5. In what ways do you show God you trust Him?

6. Record a time when you trusted God and He provided in a way only He could.

7. Mark these statements true or false:

   T   F   God is my master rather than material possessions.

   T   F   I am content with what God chooses to give me.

   T   F   I am a cheerful giver, willing to give back to God and share generously with others.

8. Why, according to Philippians 4:11-13 and Hebrews 13:5, should we be content?

9. Where do these verses tell us to draw our strength to be content from?

10. Read the following verses and record what God says to you about giving through each:

    Proverbs 3:9

    Acts 20:35

    2 Corinthians 9:7

    Philippians 2:3b-4

11. Recall a time you experienced joy when you gave to another. What made giving joyful?

Mentors

1. Read Titus 2:3-5. List the older women's qualities.

2. Think of an older woman you admire. Which qualities from your list do you see lived out in her life?

3. What do you think it means to be reverent in the way we live?

4. The Titus 2 mentor is instructed to teach what is good. What is "good teaching" according to Mark 16:15 and Philippians 4:8?

5. How have other women inspired you to love your husband, children, and home?

6. What is the ultimate goal of the Titus 2 woman?

7. According to Deuteronomy 11:18-19, what must happen in our own lives before we can teach others how to live?

8. When do you think preparation for becoming a Titus 2 woman begins?

9. If you are without a godly mentor, you can go to the Bible to discover how to live a godly life. Look up 1 Samuel 2:1-10 and Luke 1:46-55. How are Mary's and Hannah's songs similar? Do you think this is a coincidence, or could it be that Mary had read or heard Hannah's song?

10. What was Paul's admonition in Philippians 4:9? What adjustments would you need to make before you could say the words of this verse and mean them?

Friendships

1. The misuse of the tongue is one of the greatest destroyers of friendships. What does Titus 2:3-5 say is characteristic of a godly woman's words? What is uncharacteristic?

2. Can you think of a time when your words or the words of someone else maligned the cause of Christ?

3. Read James 3:1-9. In what ways are the three items to which James compares the tongue similar? What is the cause of slander or gossip, according to James 3:16?

4. Let's look in Numbers 12:1-2 at two people who used words to put someone down and to raise themselves up.

   What was Miriam and Aaron's motive in trying to stir up trouble?

   Who heard the gossip besides the Israelites? (12:4-9)

   What did God ask Miriam and Aaron?

How did God feel toward Miriam and Aaron?

What did Aaron call their slanderous words in verse 11?

Miriam was struck with leprosy for seven days. How did this affect the journey of the people? (12:15)

5. Can you recall a situation where someone's slanderous tongue caused a temporary halt in another person's spiritual journey?

6. In what ways is gossip destructive according to the following verses?

   Proverbs 11:9

   Proverbs 16:28

   Proverbs 17:9

   Proverbs 26:22

7. How can we stop gossip?

   Proverbs 17:27-28

   Proverbs 18:13

   Proverbs 26:20

   James 3:2-18

8. One of my favorite verses is Job 40:4, "I put my hand over my mouth" (NIV). Can you recall a time you should have followed that advice?

The Neighborhood and Beyond

1. Read Matthew 5:13.

   a. What does salt do?

   b. How are Christians like salt?

   c. How can you be like salt in your community?

2. Read Matthew 5:14-16.

   a. What does light do?

   b. How can you be like light in your community?

   c. How can you be like light in the world?

3. How were the following women salt and light in their communities?

Deborah—Judges 4:4-5.

Mary and Martha—Luke 10:38-39.

The woman at the well—John 4:28-42.

Dorcas—Acts 9:36-42.

Eunice—Acts 16:1; 1 Timothy 1:5.

Priscilla—Acts 18:2-3, 18, 24-26. How did she help spread the gospel? (1 Corinthians 16:19)

4. Read Isaiah 58:6-12.

   a. List the ways God suggests helping those in need.

   b. List the promises that follow.

   c. What happens when a garden is well watered (verse 11)?

5. Mary and Martha reached out to their neighbors. The Samaritan woman reached out to her town. However, Queen Esther ministered to an entire nation. Scan the book of Esther.

a. How did Esther end up as the king's wife, according to Esther 2:2-9?

b. What was her national heritage?

c. Explain the decree that Haman urged the king to sign (3:4-9).

d. Mordecai, Esther's cousin, urged her to intercede for her people with the king. However, going before the king without being summoned could result in punishment by death. When she voiced her fear to her uncle, what was his reply (4:14)?

Esther gathered her courage and called her court to pray and fast.

e. What was her reply to Mordecai (4:16)?

f. Because of her courage and dependence on God, an entire nation was saved. In what ways does Esther's story speak to you?

LESSON 14

The Neighborhood and Beyond

1. As you read the following verses, write down the specific plans God had for two of His children.

   Jeremiah 1:5

   Genesis 45:4-7

2. According to Psalm 139:13-16, what does God have planned for you?

3. When did God come up with His plan for the work you are to do (Ephesians 2:10)?

4. When God called Moses to lead the people of Israel, Moses argued fiercely. What were his arguments as to why God had the wrong man for the job (Exodus 3:11,13; 4:1,10)?

5. What was God's response to Moses at each turn (3:12, 14; 4:2-5, 11-12)?

6. What was Paul's response to his own weaknesses (2 Corinthians 12:9-10)?

7. What did God say to reassure Zechariah (Zechariah 4:6)?

8. Who is God looking for to serve Him (Isaiah 66:2)?

9. Sometimes God doesn't show us His entire plan but just enough to see if we'll obey. Read the following and note how much information His followers were given.

   a. Mark 14:13-15

   b. Genesis 12:1-3

   c. Joshua 6:2-5

   d. What would have happened if each of these individuals had said no to God?

10. What assurance does God give in Deuteronomy 31:6 for those reluctant to respond to His call?

11. The disciples were so afraid when Jesus was arrested that they scattered in every direction and hid. However, in Acts 2 we see Peter preaching boldly. What made the difference in Peter's life (Acts 2:1-4)? What does Ephesians 1:13-14 tell us about that power's availability today?

We all love maps, don't we? We like to know the plan. I've noticed that Jesus' disciples never asked Him what was next. They just stayed close to Him and joined Him in His work. What a lesson for us. Do you want to know the way? It is found in John 14:6. Don't spend too much time trying to figure out God's call on your life. Simply spend time with Him. Then, when you know He's leading you into the community or beyond, follow His mother's advice in John 2:5.

Notes

Epigraph

1. Anne Ortlund, *The Gentle Ways of the Beautiful Woman* (New York: Inspiration Press, 1998), 278.

Chapter 4

1. Henry Blackaby and Richard Blackaby, *Experiencing God Devotional* (Nashville: Broadman and Holman, 1997), 276.

Splashes from John

1. W. E. Vine, Merrill F. Unger, and William White Jr., *Vine's Complete Expository Dictionary of Old and New Testament Words* (Nashville: Nelson, 1985), 50.

Chapter 8

1. Anabel Gillham, *The Confident Woman* (Eugene, Oreg.: Harvest House, 1993), 206.
2. Roy Maynard, "Fatherhood Canceled in Primetime TV," *World,* May 20, 2000, 34.
3. Ibid., 35.
4. Ibid., 25.
5. Ibid., 22-23.
6. Sheldon Vanauken, *Under the Mercy* (San Francisco: Ignatius Press, 1985), 194-95.

Chapter 9

1. Linda Dillow and Lorraine Pintus, *Intimate Issues* (Colorado Springs: WaterBrook, 1999), 45.
2. Bob and Rosemary Barnes, *Great Sexpectations* (Grand Rapids: Zondervan, 1996), 147
3. Gail Hoch, "The Secrets of Highly Orgasmic Women," *Redbook,* November 1996, 101.

Chapter 10

1. Sheldon Vanauken, *A Severe Mercy* (New York: Bantam Books, 1977), 27.
2. Willard F. Harley Jr., *His Needs, Her Needs* (Grand Rapids: Revell, 1986), 10.
3. Bob and Rosemary Barnes, *Rock-Solid Marriage* (Grand Rapids: Zondervan, 1993), 184.
4. James Dobson, *Solid Answers* (Wheaton, Ill.: Tyndale, 1997), 480.
5. John Roseman, "Promise Keepers Challenges Husbands, But What About Wives?" *The Charlotte Observer,* February 10, 1998, 6E.
6. Ibid.

Chapter 11

1. Bob and Rosemary Barnes, *Rock-Solid Marriage* (Grand Rapids: Zondervan, 1993), 17.
2. Donna Otto, *The Gentle Art of Mentoring* (Eugene, Oreg.: Harvest House, 1997), 66-67.

Chapter 12

1. Jan Karon, *At Home in Mitford* (Elgin, Ill.: Lion Publishing, 1994), 314.
2. Mike Yorkey, ed., *Growing Healthy Families* (Brentwood, Tenn.: Wolgemuth and Hyatt, 1990), 40.
3. Ibid.

Chapter 14

1. "Information from Focus on the Family: Six Suggestions for Raising the IQ of Your Child," December 1994.

Chapter 16

1. Lysa TerKeurst, *Living Life on Purpose* (Chicago: Moody, 2000), 133-34.
2. Mortimer B. Zuckerman, "Attention Must Be Paid," *U.S. News & World Report,* August 25, 1997, 92.

Chapter 17

1. Sharon Jaynes, *Being a Great Mom, Raising Great Kids* (Chicago: Moody, 2000), 18.
2. W. E. Vine, Merrill F. Unger, and William White Jr., *Vine's Complete Expository Dictionary of Old and New Testament Words* (Nashville: Nelson, 1985), 282.
3. Jaynes, *Being a Great Mom,* 25.
4. Kay Willis and Mary Ann Buckmum Brinley, "Sixteen Ways to Listen to Your Child," *Good Housekeeping,* August 1998, 158.
5. Robert C. Crosby, *Now We're Talking! Questions That Bring You Closer to Your Kids* (Colorado Springs: Focus on the Family, 1996), xii.
6. Jaynes, *Being a Great Mom,* 75.
7. Ibid., 76.
8. Ibid., 66.
9. Ibid., 151.
10. Ibid., 160, 165.
11. Caroline Brownlow, comp., *Dear Mom: A Book of Loving Thoughts* (Ft. Worth: Brownlow Corp., 1999).
12. Jaynes, *Being a Great Mom,* 186.
13. Gilda Radner, *It's Always Something* (New York: Avon Books, 1989), 268-69.

Chapter 20

1. Emilie Barnes with Anne Christian Buchanan, *Welcome Home* (Eugene, Oreg.: Harvest House, 1997), 120.
2. Spiros Zodhiates, *The Hebrew-Greek Key Study Bible* (Chattanooga, Tenn.: AMG Publishers, 1990), 1609.

Chapter 21

1. Liz Curtis Higgs, *Only Angels Can Wing It* (Nashville: Nelson, 1995), 108.
2. Adapted from "What to Do with a Piece of Paper," Ann Marie Peterson, *The Proverbs 31 Newsletter,* January 2000, 6.
3. Sharon Jaynes, *Becoming a Woman Who Listens to God* (Eugene, Oreg: Harvest House Publishers, 2004), 70.

Chapter 22

1. Tracy Porter, *Returning Home* (Kansas City, Kan.: Andrews & McMeel, 1997), 1-2.

Chapter 24

1. *The Life Application Bible* (Wheaton, Ill.: Tyndale, 1988), 1338.

CHAPTER 25

1. Kevin Leman, *Bonkers* (New York: Dell, 1987), 188.
2. Liz Curtis Higgs, *Only Angels Can Wing It* (Nashville: Nelson, 1995), 108.

CHAPTER 26

1. Ron and Judy Blue, *Money Talks and So Should We* (Grand Rapids: Zondervan, 1999), 12.
2. Kathy Bergen, "Richer but Not Happier," *The Charlotte Observer,* September 10, 2000, D1.
3. Ibid.
4. Ibid.
5. *Crown Ministries Small Group Financial Study* (Longwood, Fla.: Crown Ministries, 1986), 23.
6. Ibid., 42.
7. Bob and Rosemary Barnes, *Rock-Solid Marriage* (Grand Rapids: Zondervan, 1993), 145.
8. Willard F. Harley Jr., *His Needs, Her Needs* (Grand Rapids: Revell, 1986), 10.
9. *Crown Ministries,* 27.
10. Ibid.

CHAPTER 30

1. Win Couchman, "Cross-Generational Relationships," talk at Women for Christ conference, 1983.
2. Susan Hunt, *Spiritual Mothering* (Franklin, Tenn.: Legacy Communications, 1992), 67.
3. Ibid., 12.

CHAPTER 31

1. Dee Brestin, *The Friendships of Women* (Wheaton, Ill.: Victor, 1988), 165.
2. Hans Christian Andersen, *The Snow Queen* (New York: Grosset and Dunlap, 1981).
3. Brestin, *Friendships,* 120.

CHAPTER 34

1. Mary Lance Sisk, *Love Your Neighbor as Yourself: Blessing Your Neighborhood Through Love and Prayer* (self-published, 1999), 43-44.
2. Gustav Niebuhr and Laurie Goodstein, "Who Will Be the Next Billy Graham?" *The Charlotte Observer,* January 2, 1999, 15A.

CHAPTER 35

1. Beth Moore, *Praying God's Word* (Nashville: Broadman & Holman, 2000), 159.

SPLASHES FROM JOHN 7

1. Kenneth L. Barker and John R. Kohlenberger III, consulting eds., *Zondervan NIV Bible Commentary* (Grand Rapids: Zondervan, 1994), 319.

CHAPTER 36

1. "Everest: Mountain Without Mercy," *Turning Point,* Sept. 19, 1996.
2. Dr. Seaborn "Beck" Weathers, "Left for Dead," *National Geographic,* [online]. (1997). Available: http://www.nationalgeographic.com/books/9710/left.html.

About Proverbs 31 Ministries

Proverbs 31 Ministries is a nondenominational organization dedicated to glorifying God by touching women's hearts to build godly homes. Through Jesus Christ, we shed light on God's distinctive design for women and the great responsibilities we have been given. With Proverbs 31:10-31 as a guide, we encourage and equip women to practice living out their faith as wives, mothers, friends, and neighbors.

What began in 1992 as a monthly newsletter has now grown into a multi-faceted ministry reaching women across the country and around the globe. Each aspect of the ministry seeks to equip women in the Seven Principles of the **Proverbs 31 Woman.**

1. The Proverbs 31 woman reveres Jesus Christ as Lord of her life and pursues an ongoing, personal relationship with Him.

2. The Proverbs 31 woman loves, honors, and respects her husband as the leader of the home.

3. The Proverbs 31 woman nurtures her children and believes that motherhood is a high calling with the responsibility of shaping and molding the children who will one day define who we are as a community and a nation.

4. The Proverbs 31 woman is a disciplined and industrious keeper of the home who creates a warm and loving environment for her family and friends.

5. The Proverbs 31 woman contributes to the financial well-being of her household by being a faithful steward of time and money God has entrusted to her.

6. The Proverbs 31 woman speaks with wisdom and faithful instruction as she mentors and supports other women, and develops godly friendships.

7. The Proverbs 31 woman shares the love of Christ by extending her hands to help with the needs in the community.

Ministry Features

Through a monthly magazine, *P31 Woman,* an international daily radio program, dynamic speakers with life-changing messages, on-line communities and on-line daily devotions, Proverbs 31 Ministries seeks to help women discover a passion for Jesus Christ, define their purpose as a wife, mother, mentor, and friend, and develop a godly perspective on womanhood based on biblical principles.

To learn more about Proverbs 31 Ministries, visit www.proverbs31.org. To inquire about having Lysa TerKeurst or Sharon Jaynes speak at your women's event, contact them at lysa@proverbs31.org or sharon@sharonjaynes.com.